A2-Level Business Studies

The Revision Guide

Exam Board: AQA

Editors:
Gemma Hallam, Katherine Reed

Contributors:
P. M. Brockbank, John Grant, Peter Gray, Jeff Harris, Jane Hosking,
Nagu Rao, David Morris, Adrian Murray, Lynda Turner, Keith Williamson

Proofreaders:
Keri Barrow, Ellen Bowness, Victoria Skelton

Published by Coordination Group Publications Ltd.

ISBN: 1 84146 393 0
Groovy website: www.cgpbooks.co.uk
Jolly bits of clipart from CorelDRAW
Printed by Elanders Hindson, Newcastle upon Tyne.

Contents

We deliberately haven't put any essay answers in this book, because they'd just be repeating what's in the revision guide. Instead, we've put in a section about how to write good essay answers, and do well. Answers for the numerical questions are included though, on page 98.

Marketing

You've covered some marketing at AS level — there's more to learn for A2, though.

The **Role** of **Marketing** is to **Identify** and **Satisfy** customer **Needs and Wants**

1) Market research and analysis finds out what customers **need and want**. Marketing also tries to **anticipate** what they'll want in the future so that the business can get an advantage over its competitors.
2) Marketing tries to ensure that the business supplies goods and services that the customer **wants**, in order to **maximise profit**. It's mutually beneficial for the business and the customer — the customer gets something they like, the business makes a profit.
3) Remember, marketing covers **market research**, **market analysis**, **market planning** and the "**marketing mix**" — the four big Ps of product, price, promotion and place (distribution).

Marketing affects all **Departments** and **Functions** in a business

1) Most larger businesses have a specialised **marketing department** — but marketing affects **all departments**.
2) **Market analysis** can tell the **finance** department **how much** the business is likely to make in **sales**. Market analysis tells the business how **big** the market for a product is, so they know if they can **expand** and make more profits without having to **diversify** into supplying new products.
3) Market research and analysis tells the **research and development** people what kind of products to **research** and **design**, in order to meet **future needs**.

1) Marketing is also **influenced** by other business functions.
2) For example, the business' **marketing budget** is influenced by its overall **financial position** — when money's tight, the marketing budget will be small.
3) Also, any changes in production capacity or human resources affect the business' **strengths** and **weaknesses**, which affect the **marketing strategy** it chooses to follow.

Marketing objectives may **conflict** with the objectives of other departments. For example, the production department may want to continue with the same processes that they've always used, while the marketing department might want to diversify and make new products using new processes.

Product-led marketing **Focuses** on the **Product** rather than customer needs

1) **Product-led** businesses start by deciding what they can **produce**. They put the product ahead of customer needs or budget constraints.
2) **Product-led marketing** is a **risky** strategy, because it **assumes** that customers will love the product. Customers might want or need a **different product** altogether.
3) The product-led approach only really works when there's very **little competition** in the market, or when the product is something that customers really want.

Market-led marketing aims to **Give Customers** what they **Want**

1) **Market oriented** businesses start by finding out what the **customer wants**.
2) A **market-led** approach is more likely to **succeed** than a product-led approach.
3) The market-led approach has **risks** — it chases customer needs even when the firm doesn't have the right **resources** to meet them.
   - A market-led strategy can push a business into competitive new markets where it doesn't have enough **experience** to make the right decisions. For example, it'd be foolish for a business to enter the digital camera market without experience in consumer electronics or old fashioned film camera technology.
   - A market-led strategy can push a business into markets where it doesn't have **competitive advantage** over businesses already in the market. For example, say that market research indicates customer desire for smaller digital cameras. It'd be foolish for a business to try to produce a smaller digital camera, unless they were confident that they could do it **better** and **cheaper** than the **existing big players** in the market.
4) A business operating in a market where it doesn't have **experience** or the right **resources** can end up **overstretching** its **limited resources**, and giving **poor customer service**. This often ends in failure, with **disappointed** customers leaving the brand.

Marketing

Asset-led marketing *Matches* business *Strengths* to what *Customers Want*

1) **Asset-led marketing** combines **consumer wants** with the **strengths** and **assets** of the business. For example, when developing the **new Mini**, **BMW** linked the **market desire** for a new small car with **reliability** and engineering expertise.
2) **Asset-led marketing** has the strengths of market-led marketing, **without** the **weaknesses**. It helps businesses ensure that they're **capable** of making a product customers need before they start the manufacturing process.
3) Asset-led businesses **don't waste time and effort** on potential market opportunities when they don't have the **resources** and **experience** to succeed. They invest their time and resources in market opportunities that **match** their strength and skills.
4) Asset-led marketing is seen as the best route to long term **customer satisfaction** and **brand loyalty**. The asset-led approach gives businesses a much better chance of providing good customer service, and meeting customer needs.

Brand Image and *Reputation* are important in the *Asset-led* approach

1) The airline **easyJet** has a reputation for **cheap**, **no-frills service**, and a recognisable **brand image**. This helped them to **diversify** into other services, e.g. car rental and internet cafes. The **easy** group could offer the same cheap, no-frills service in these other areas, which gave them a **competitive advantage** — particularly when combined with customer trust in the **easy** brand.
2) BMW's **reputation** for **reliability** and good engineering was a key asset in the marketing of the **new Mini**. This gave BMW a competitive advantage over some other car manufacturers, and allowed them to charge a **premium price** for the new Mini — customers were happy to pay a premium price because they trusted the BMW brand.

Location and *Distribution* are important in the *Asset-led* approach

1) Tesco have hundreds of **supermarket branches** across the UK. This was an important asset in their decision to diversify into **personal finance** — they could offer application forms for financial products at their supermarket branches. Tesco also have a strong **website**, which offers a "one stop shop" for a very wide range of goods including groceries, DVDs, insurance and internet access. Tesco can easily offer **new services** through the website.
2) A **global brand** with a **global distribution network** could sell new products using its distribution network. For example, Coca Cola used its global distribution network to market a new brand of bottled water.

Practice Questions

Q1 How does marketing affect the finance department?

Q2 What's market-led marketing?

Q3 Give one reason why asset-led marketing is better than market-led marketing.

Exam Question

Q1 Imagine that a luxury car brand is planning to launch a range of men's toiletries and grooming products. How would you advise them to develop this kind of product using an asset-led approach? (10 marks)

Marketing — even educated fleas do it...

Product-led, market-led and asset-led marketing are all brand new for A2. Make sure you understand them. You might be asked to evaluate a market-led or asset-led approach, or you might have to characterise the marketing strategy of a business in a case study. Either way, it's useful to know the kinds of business assets that are relevant to asset-led marketing.

Market Analysis and Buyer Behaviour

Market analysis tells firms about the size of the market and the customers within the market. Firms also like to know why customers within the market buy what they buy.

Market Analysis tells firms about Market Size and Growth

Looks like a big one.

1) **Market size** is the **total** of all the **sales** within the market. It's measured by either the **volume of sales** (the **number of units** sold) or the **value of sales** (the total sales **revenue**).
2) Businesses need to know if the market is **growing** or **shrinking**.
3) **Competition** in a **shrinking** market is **heavy** — there are fewer customers to go around. Firms may want to get out of a market that's getting smaller.
4) In a **growing** market, **several** firms can **grow easily**.

Market Analysis tells firms about Market Share

1) Market share is the **percentage** of sales in a market that is made by **one firm**, or by **one brand**.
Market share = sales ÷ total market size × 100 %
2) For example, if **1 out of 4** PCs bought was a Dell, this would give Dell a **25% market share** (in terms of volume). If **£1 out of every £10** spent on perfume was a Chanel purchase, this'd give Chanel a **10% market share** (in terms of value). It's easy to work out.
3) It's important to look at **trends in market share** as well as trends in sales revenue. Letting your market share slip is not good — it means that **competitors** are **gaining advantage** over you.

Example: Say the mobile gaming market has grown by **15%** from one year to the next. A software company selling games for mobile devices would not be happy if they'd only increased sales by **5%** from £200 000 to £210 000 — they're failing to grow at the **same rate** as the market, so their **market share** has gone down. That 5% growth isn't looking so good now that they know that someone's muscling in on their market share.

Markets are Segmented into groups of Similar Customers

Different groups of customers have different needs. **Analysing** different **segments** of a market allows a firm to focus on the needs of **specific groups** within a target market. A market can be segmented in several ways:

1) **Income.** Luxury products are aimed at high income groups.
2) **Socio-economic class.** Businesses can segment their market based on the kind of jobs people have — from senior professionals to unemployed people.

A	Higher managerial, administrative and professional, e.g. hospital consultant, MD of big firm, barrister.
B	Intermediate managerial, administrative and professional, e.g. teacher, accountant.
C1	Supervisory or clerical, junior managerial/administrative/professional, e.g. production supervisor.
C2	Skilled manual, e.g. plumber, electrician, chef, hairdresser, gas fitter.
D	Semi-skilled and unskilled manual, e.g. bus driver, waiter/waitress, postman/woman, cleaner.
E	Casual labourers, state pensioners, the unemployed.

3) **Age.** Businesses target products at specific age groups — pre-teens, teens, 25-35 year olds, the over 55s etc.
4) **Gender.** For example, chocolate manufacturers target some bars at women (Flake) and some at men (Yorkie).
5) **Geographical region.** Some products have a regional market — e.g. Welsh cakes, haggis.
6) **Amount of use.** For example, mobile phone suppliers market differently to heavy users and light users.
7) **Ethnic grouping.** New ethnic minority digital TV channels make it easier for firms to target ethnic groups.
8) **Family size.** New houses are built with a number of bedrooms to suit the target consumer. Large "family packs" of breakfast cereal, loo roll etc. are aimed at large families.
9) **Lifestyle.** Busy young workers buy lots of microwavable ready meals, so ready meals are targeted at them.

All the above methods focus on a **characteristic of the customer**. In addition, new segmentation methods categorise markets according to the **reasons** for buying a product — as an essential, as a luxury, as a gift, etc.

Market Aggregation lumps all segments together as a Mass Market

Market aggregation tries to appeal to **everyone**, by marketing a product with **general appeal**, that everyone will hopefully like. It's the **opposite** of **market segmentation**, which markets products to some market segments and deliberately ignores or excludes others. Marketing has moved increasingly **away** from mass market aggregation.

Market Analysis and Buyer Behaviour

*Businesses need to **Know Their Customers** — **Why** they buy **What** they buy*

1) Understanding **why** a customer buys a product allows a business to **respond** to the **customer's needs**.
2) Psychologists study the **science of behaviour**, so psychology can provide insights into motivation. Businesses can use psychology in their marketing to subtly persuade people to buy.
3) Businesses aim to identify and anticipate **cultural shifts** which influence buying behaviour. A move towards **healthier lifestyles** has prompted growth in sales of low fat foods, gym memberships and exercise equipment.
4) Purchasers go through several **stages** when they buy something: 1) **recognising** the **need**, 2) **finding information**, 3) considering **alternatives**, 4) **purchasing** the product, and 5) **evaluating** the purchase.
5) For **low value** purchases (also called "**low involvement**" purchases), this all happens very quickly and purchasers may skip steps 2 and 3. For **high involvement**, high cost industrial contracts, the process could take **years**.

Customer Personality** affects **New Product Uptake

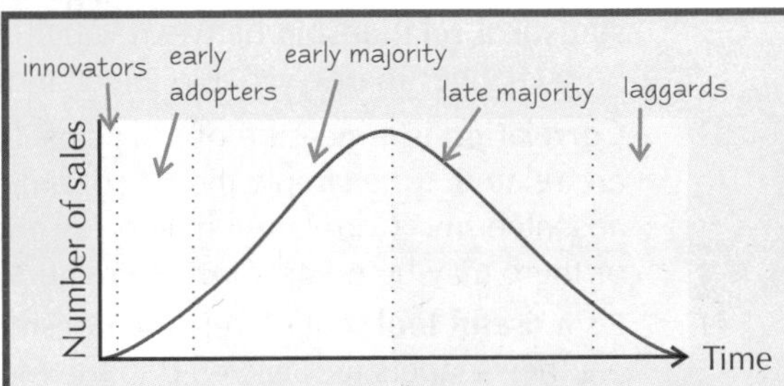

1) "**Innovators**" are the **very first** to buy the shiny new thing when it comes out. There are only a very few innovators.
2) "**Early adopters**" buy the new product **soon** after it's released. They're the sort of people who others go to for **advice** on what digital camera to buy, what sort of espresso maker to get, etc.
3) "**Early majority**" buyers buy **fashionable** stuff before it goes out of fashion, but they're more conservative than early adopters.
4) "**Late majority**" buyers are **sceptical** of new technology and want to be sure that it'll work and that it won't break.
5) "**Laggards**" are **behind** everyone else — **everyone's** got one by now, **except** this lot. For example, they couldn't imagine what they'd want a mobile phone for. They tend to be nostalgic about the past.

Customers** can play **Different Roles** in **Purchasing

There can be more than one customer in each purchase — purchaser and decision maker both count as customers.

In any purchase, a customer plays **one or more** of these **roles**.

1) The **initiator** gets the ball rolling, and decides that there's a need to buy.
2) The **influencer** tries to influence the decider or the purchaser. **Kids** are often influencers.
3) The **gatekeeper** is the person who stands in between a sales person and a decision maker. For example, a **secretary** can decide whether to give a photocopier rep an **appointment** with the boss.
4) The **decision maker** makes the decision to buy, obviously.
5) The **purchaser** is the one who actually does the buying. In a **domestic** purchase, the decision maker and purchaser are usually the **same person**. In an **industrial** purchase, a **manager** usually makes the decision to buy, and a **purchase clerk** does the actual purchase order.
6) The **user** is the one who actually uses the thing. If they're lucky, they'll have some input into the purchase.

Practice Questions

Q1 Give examples of four different ways that markets are segmented.

Q2 What's the difference between market segmentation and market aggregation?

Q3 What are the five stages a buyer goes through when making a purchase?

Q4 What are the six roles identified in a purchase?

Exam Questions

Q1 Knowledge of customers is the most important factor for a small business making handmade jewellery. Discuss. (12 marks)

Q2 Analyse the use of psychology in marketing reduced calorie chocolate bars. (8 marks)

The orange market — all too easily segmented...

Blimey, there's a lot on these pages. Some of it follows on from AS work, so it shouldn't be totally new. Market segmentation and buyer behaviour kind of go together. You can segment based on gender, age, class etc., and you can make assumptions about the buyer behaviour of those segments. You can also segment based on psychology.

Marketing Analysis

Businesses need to be able to analyse market data, to figure out what it all means.

Some marketing analysis uses **Qualitative Techniques**

1) **Qualitative** techniques involve **human judgement** rather than maths and calculation. They're particularly useful when there's **not much data** to go on, and when the time frame being investigated is long.
2) The main qualitative techniques used are **panel consensus** (See **Delphi** technique on p.13), **personal insight** and using **historical analogies** — i.e. drawing on past experiences.

Causal Methods are **Quantitative Techniques** which use **Maths** and **Correlation**

1) **Causal** methods use **mathematical models** and **correlation** to figure out a **cause and effect** relationship. An example of something that suits this technique is price elasticity of demand, which measures how demand for goods responds to a change in price.
2) Using **mathematical models** managers can establish a **statistical relationship** between variables and forecast how changes in one variable affect another.
3) **Correlation** is a measure of how **closely** two variables are **related**, for example the pay of employees and their absenteeism. Correlation may be **strong** (high), **weak**, or there may be no apparent correlation at all.

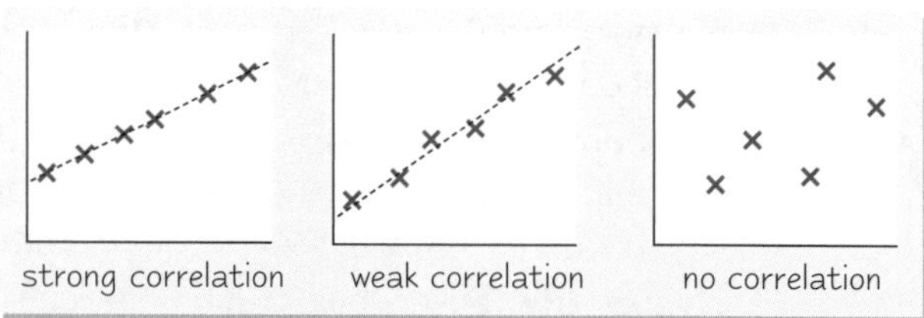

4) It's a **useful tool**, but correlation **doesn't prove** cause and effect by itself. **Other variables** may be important — e.g. newspapers are delivered in the morning, but the sunrise doesn't make the paper fall on the doormat.

Time Series Analysis records data over **Time**

1) **Time series analysis** is used to reveal **underlying patterns** by recording and plotting data over time, for example the recording of **sales** over a year.
2) **Trends** are the long-term movement of a variable, for example the sales of a particular product over a number of years. Trends may be **upward**, **constant** or **downward**, but there are usually **fluctuations** around the trend.
3) **Seasonal** fluctuations repeat on a **regular** daily, weekly or yearly basis, e.g. the use of electricity over a 24-hour period, or the sale of ice lollies over a year.
4) **Cyclical** fluctuations are regular repetitions over a **medium term** period, often many years. The business cycle of boom and bust has a cyclical pattern.

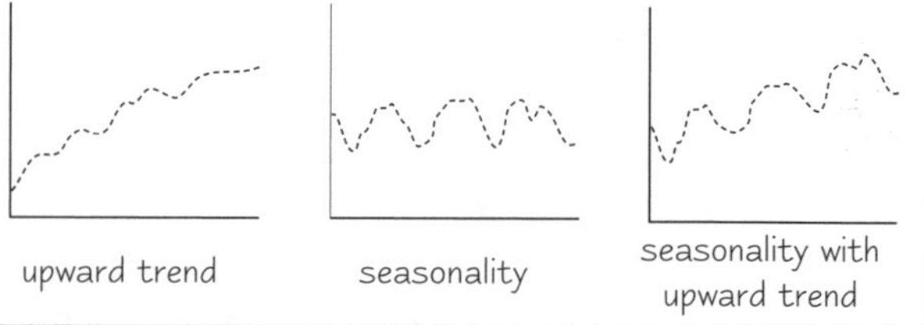

5) **Random** fluctuations can be completely random. They also include the results of **major disturbances** — things like **war**, changes of government and sudden **unpredictable events** like the terrorist acts of 9/11, the outbreak of foot and mouth disease or the 2004 Asian tsunami.

Data can be **Extrapolated** to **Predict** the **Future**

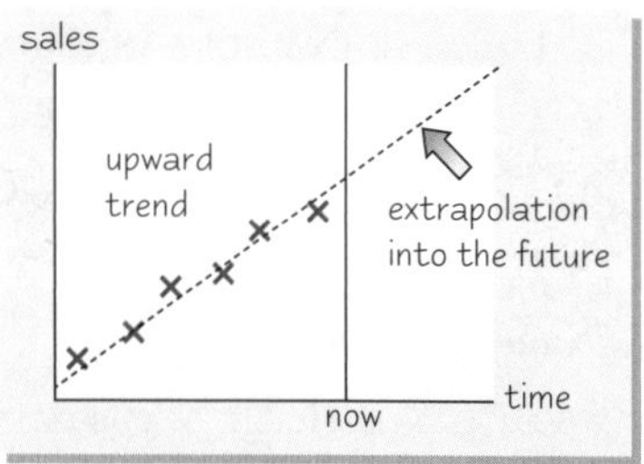

1) The pattern revealed by data can be **extended** into the **future**.
2) Managers identify the **trend**, and **assume** the trend will carry on into the future.
3) For example, a graph of sales figures over time can show correlation between sales and time — say an upwards trend. All you do to **extrapolate** is draw a line of best fit on the graph to show the trend, and keep the line going to project the trend into the future. Then you read off the predicted sales figures. Easy.
4) Extrapolation works great with **constant trends**. Unfortunately, the **pace of change** in the market can be very fast. **Customer desires** and **technological advances** change quickly. This means that extrapolations from the past don't always predict the future very accurately.
5) **Sudden unexpected events** are the biggest pitfall for extrapolation. Random fluctuations in the market due to things like **natural disasters** make extrapolation from past data look completely useless. For example, extrapolation from sales of beef in the UK in the 1980s would predict a healthy, growing market. In the 1990s, the BSE crisis meant that everything turned belly up.

Marketing Analysis

*A **Moving Average** is **Updated** as **New Information** is received*

1) A **moving average** is one which is recalculated as new information comes in, to give you up to date information. E.g. the **inflation** rate, which is an **average** of the previous **twelve months**' price rises, is **updated every month**.
2) The effect of a moving average is to **smooth out data** and isolate underlying **trends** from seasonal, cyclical and random **fluctuations**. Once the trend has been isolated it can be **extrapolated** on a graph.

*An example of **Moving Averages** — pay attention because it's **Tough***

Step 1 Work out the total for the **first 4 quarters**. Put it in the **4 quarter moving total** column, in the **Q4 of 2001** row.

Step 2 Work out the total for the **next 4 quarters** (2001 Q2 to 2002 Q1), and put it in the 4 quarter moving total column, beside Q1 of 2002. **Repeat** this process for the next 4 quarters, and the next, till you're done.

Step 3 Add the **4 quarter moving total** for **2001 Q4** and the 4 quarter moving total for **2002 Q1** and put it in the **8 quarter moving total column**, in the 2002 Q1 row. **Repeat** for the rest of the 4 quarter totals.

You do this because the average calculated in Step 1 doesn't line up with any of the quarters — it lines up with a point between Q2 and Q3 of 2001. Adding the two 4 quarter totals together takes data from 5 quarters, with quarters 2001 Q2, Q3 and Q4 appearing twice. Because it covers 5 quarters, it's got a proper midpoint. If you were doing a 3 month moving average, you wouldn't have to bother with this.

Year	Quarter	Sales revenue (thousand £s)	4 quarter moving total	8 quarter moving total	Quarterly moving average
2001	1	243			
	2	250			
	3	289			261.00
	4	256	1038		264.63
2002	1	255	1050	2088	268.38
	2	267	1067	2117	270.00
	3	302	1080	2147	271.50
	4	256	1080	2160	274.25
2003	1	267	1092	2172	276.50
	2	277	1102	2194	284.88
	3	310	1110	2212	290.13
	4	315	1169	2279	
2004	1	250	1152	2321	

Step 4 **Divide** the **8 quarter total** by **8**, put the value in the **quarterly moving average** column in the 2001 Q3 row.

Step 5 **Repeat** this process for the rest of the **8 quarter totals**. This gives you your quarterly moving averages.

Moving Averages** have **Limitations

1) Moving averages are **difficult** to work out over long periods.
2) They're **no use at all** in **unstable** environments.
3) The **past** isn't always a good basis for predicting the future.
4) More recent data should be **weighted** to make it more important.
5) The periods should **match the business cycle** to capture up and down turns.

Practice Questions

Q1 What is correlation?

Q2 What is extrapolation?

Q3 What are moving averages?

Q4 What is time series analysis?

Exam Questions

Q1 a) Calculate the quarterly moving average trend for the sales revenue data below (figures are in thousands). (14 marks)

2001 Q1	630	2002 Q1	621	2003 Q1	602	2004 Q1	589
Q2	567	Q2	578	Q2	550		
Q3	552	Q3	543	Q3	502		
Q4	678	Q4	600	Q4	560		

The answers to these questions are on p.98.

b) Plot the Quarterly Moving Average trend on a graph. (6 marks)

These moving averages can reach quite a speed on level ground...

Those moving averages are hard to get your head round, but not impossible. You'll need to really make sure that you genuinely, honestly follow all the steps for calculating them. Don't kid yourself that you get it if you don't. Read the hints for each step, and you can understand it. Honest. It's doable. Don't be tempted to skip it, because it may be in the exam.

Marketing Decision-Making

Marketing involves making difficult decisions.

***Marketing** is about **Making Decisions** to suit the market*

1) Marketing isn't just about market research, or marketing activity. It's about **making decisions** and making sure that all the necessary **resources** are in place to allow the business to take the **right action**.
2) It's often very **hard** for managers to come to the right marketing decisions. Markets are constantly evolving — **consumers' needs** change and develop and the rapid pace of technological change creates **uncertainties**. It's **not easy** to figure out what the market for mobile phones, handheld games or even women's sports shoes will be like in 5 years' time.

***Scientific Marketing** is a **Systematic** approach*

1) The **scientific marketing model** attempts to **eliminate guesswork** and **bias**. It does this by emphasising **objective** decision-making and the use of **factual** and **numerical** data.
2) The model consists of a series of **stages**: setting **objectives**, **gathering data**, **analysing** data, forming a **hypothesis** (a **marketing strategy**), **testing** it out, **evaluating** it and then **changing** the strategy if necessary.
3) It's **scientific** because marketers examine a hypothesis, consider alternatives and analyse results, just like **scientists** do.
4) **Market research** is **fundamental** to the procedure — it's impossible to form a hypothesis or test it without **good data**.
5) There's also wide use of **quantitative data**, **statistical analysis** and **mathematical modelling**, for example calculating and modelling price elasticity by looking at the correlation between price and demand.

Set objectives → Gather data → Analyse data → Form a strategy → Try it out → Evaluate how it worked → Set objectives

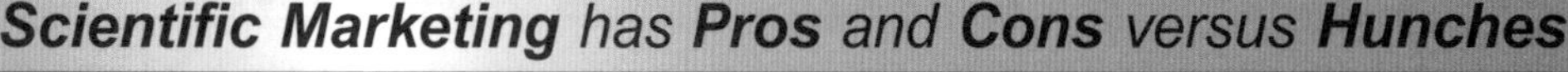

Scientific Marketing** has **Pros** and **Cons** versus **Hunches

1) The scientific method is only as **reliable** as the **data** that it uses. **Dodgy market research** gives **dodgy data**, which gives **dodgy decisions**.
2) Market research data can be **difficult** or **expensive** to come up with. It may be more **practical** to rely on **past experience** or **hunches**, rather than going to the far end of the earth to find out the data. In a stable market, when there's lots of time to figure out a decision, the scientific method is best.
3) Hunches are very **risky** because they aren't based on rational thought or quantifiable data. However, the more **experience** a manager has, the better their decisions are likely to be. **Experience** can fine-tune hunches.
4) The scientific method gives more reliable results, but it tends to churn out boring, predictable decisions. When management want an off-the-wall creative solution, it makes sense to make decisions based on hunches.
5) **Small firms** operating in **niche markets** do not have the **resources** or **specialist skills** to properly make use of the scientific model. New small businesses don't have enough **experience** to fall back on, either. This "double whammy" is one of the reasons for the high **failure** rate of new businesses.

Marketing Managers** use the **AIDA Model** to develop **Promotional Campaigns

1) The **AIDA** model is used to develop promotional campaigns. It's mainly applied to **above-the-line** activities such as **advertising** through the media, although it can be applied to below-the-line promotion.
2) The idea behind the **AIDA** model is that **effective advertising** goes through **four stages**:

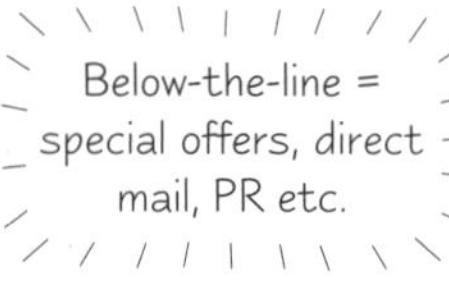

1) **A**ttention	First, the advertiser aims to grab the consumer's **attention**. An **amusing** or **controversial** ad campaign works well for this.
2) **I**nterest	Next, the advertiser aims to get the consumer **interested** in the product. The ads try to **differentiate** the brand from rival brands.
3) **D**esire	The focus is on **persuading** the consumer he or she **wants the product**. Advertising may portray a **desirable image**. **Free samples** may be offered.
4) **A**ct	The aim now is to get the consumer to **act** and **actually buy** the product. **Sales promotions** (e.g. low initial price, three for price of two) are often used.

Marketing Decision-Making

DAGMAR is a model for Promotion and Advertising

1) **DAGMAR** stands for **D**efining **A**dvertising **G**oals for **M**easured **A**dvertising **R**esults.
2) DAGMAR aims to **increase awareness** of the product. It's based on the idea that **customers** move through a series of **five stages** when buying a product.

Stage	Consumer	Promotion
Unawareness	**Doesn't know** about the product.	Media advertising.
Awareness	Has a **vague awareness** of the product.	Media advertising.
Comprehension	**Recognises** and **knows about** the product.	Support through product information.
Conviction	**Prefers** the product to others.	Advertising to reinforce brand differentiation.
Action	**Purchases** the product (hooray).	Personal selling.

3) The **promotional mix** is designed to move the customer **smoothly** through the stages.
4) The DAGMAR model follows the psychological pattern of **buyer behaviour**, (see p.5). For **impulse**, or **low-value** sales (e.g. an ice-cream) the customer may blend stages together, and recognise and understand the product as soon as they're aware of it, which lets them take action quickly. For **high value** sales, the process of increasing awareness can take months.
5) Some things stop the consumer from moving through the five stages — competitor activity, unwillingness to buy and memory lapses can all slow things down.

Promotional mix = the different sorts of promotion used.

Ansoff's Matrix is used for Strategic Decisions

1) Ansoff's Matrix is used to analyse a business' **markets** and **products**.
2) **Market penetration** involves selling the same goods to the same market. The aim is to **encourage greater use** amongst existing users, or to prompt users of rival products to **switch brand**. It's not risky.
3) **Product development** is selling **new products** to **existing markets**. It's used when the market has good **growth potential** and the business has high market share, strong R&D and a good **competitive advantage**.
4) **Market development** is selling **existing products** to **new markets**, for example **new market segments**, or **new geographical areas**. It's particularly relevant to **product-led businesses** with considerable **production assets**, who can easily make lots of identical products and sell them in new areas. Market development can be **risky**, unless the firm has spotted a **clear new market opportunity**.
5) **Diversification** involves selling **new products** to **new markets**. Diversification is a **very risky** strategy. It's appropriate when a business really needs to diversify to reduce dependence on a **limited product range**, when there's promise of **high profits**, or when the company has **cash reserves** to fall back on.

Markets \ Products	Existing	New
Existing	Market penetration	Product development
New	Market extension or development	Diversification

Businesses also use SWOT Analysis for marketing decision-making

The SWOT model is covered in the **AS book**, and it's also covered on **p.90** of this book. So go check it out.

Practice Questions

Q1 List the steps in the AIDA model.

Q2 What are the stages a customer needs to be moved through in the DAGMAR model?

Q3 Outline the 4 parts of Ansoff's Matrix.

Q4 Why might a business seek to diversify?

Exam Question

Q1 Explain two problems a business that designs electronic games might face if it makes marketing decisions based solely on the scientific marketing model. (6 marks)

Follow your gut feeling — my gut says "have a ham sandwich"...

It's a bit odd that you're expected to seriously weigh up "scientific method" versus "oh, well, just guess". Thing is, it isn't as simple as that. The data you'd use for a scientific marketing approach might not be very good. An experienced business person who's been there, done that and bought the T-shirt doesn't always need to work everything out with a pencil.

Marketing Planning

Obviously, businesses have to plan everything, especially their marketing activities.

Marketing Planning is about turning Objectives into Action

1) Marketing planning sets out a **coordinated action plan** for operations, finance and personnel functions, so that they meet the firm's **corporate** and **marketing** objectives. Marketing plans **integrate business functions together**.
2) A marketing plan provides **background information** into the nature of the business and its markets, describes the **marketing strategies** that'll be employed and the **detailed action plans** and **budgets** that those strategies need.
3) Some people describe marketing as the **interface** between the **customer's needs** and the **other management functions**. Marketing is the central, **integrating** function which makes sure that the products provided meet the customer's needs — in terms of **specification**, **price**, **availability** etc.

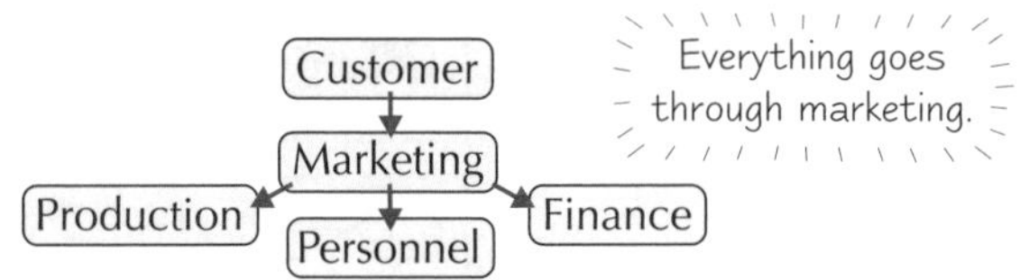

4) There's a **trade-off** between meeting the **customer's needs** and **making profit**. **Asset-led marketing** (see p.3) acknowledges that businesses need to **play to their strengths** and utilise their assets effectively, so it's the best placed to please the customer and the finance department at the same time.
5) Hugh Davidson is a marketing guru who believes that marketing concerns **everybody** within a business and it's **everyone's responsibility** to build **added value** on behalf of the customer. His ideas of what marketing should do to make sure it turns objectives into results are summarised as **POISE**:

Profitable	Marketing must balance value to the **customer** with **profitability**.
Offensive	Marketing needs to be **proactive**, take **risks** and **invest** for the long term.
Integrated	Marketing is **everyone's responsibility**, in **every department** of the business.
Strategic	Marketing should be done after **careful analysis** and evaluation of alternatives.
Effectively communicated	Marketing requires **commitment** and **cooperation** from **all staff** and departments.

A marketing plan Asks Questions... and Answers them

In order to develop a marketing plan a business needs to ask and answer some **key questions** about itself, including:

Question the business must ask...	**How to answer it**
Where are we **now**?	Do a **market audit**.
Where do we **want** to go?	Set **corporate objectives**. Set **marketing objectives**.
How will we get there?	Devise **strategies** – broad methods. Plan **tactics** – specific, detailed plans.
How do we **know** when we've **arrived**?	**Evaluate progress**, compare progress with **measurable targets**.

"What plan was behind this vile knitwear?" pondered Chandra Funnel, the great marketing detective.

Marketing Plans are Great, but they can Go Wrong

Marketing plans are great because...

Developing a marketing plan **focuses marketing activity**, provides a **plan** for **all departments**, picks out marketing **opportunities** and **anticipates** potential problems.

Strategic marketing planning aims to cope with change — but sometimes it fails to cope.

Strategic planning **anticipates change**, provides clear objectives and **direction** and encourages **effective planning**. The process of **analysis** improves **understanding** of the market. But... the **fast pace of change** may render plans redundant. Also, if strategies are **vague** and the information used is **out of date**, they won't cope well with future changes.

Marketing plans can go wrong when...

The **business functions aren't well integrated**, managers are **short-term in outlook**, **bureaucracy** overwhelms the planning process, there isn't enough good **market research** or **analysis**, the **business culture** resists taking **responsibility** for marketing, there isn't enough **working capital** to pay for the best strategies.

Marketing Planning

The marketing planning Process is Cyclical

1) Setting **goals**:	**Mission statement** and overall **corporate objectives**.
2) **Analysing** the situation:	**Marketing audit**, **SWOT** analysis, marketing **assumptions**.
3) Coming up with **strategy**:	Marketing **objectives** and **strategy**. **Forecast** of expected **results**, **target** setting. **Alternative plans** in case things **change**.
4) **Allocating resources**:	**Marketing budget** and **detailed action plan**.
5) **Monitoring** and **adjusting** strategy:	**Checking performance** against **targets**. **Adjusting** if necessary.

Back to step 3.

Analysis and Audits look at Internal and External Factors and Trends

1) A market audit is an appraisal of **internal** and **external** factors affecting the business, e.g:

Business Environment	The Market	Internal Audit	Competition
Political and Legal Economic Social Technical International	Size and growth Segments Buyer habits Cost of entry Opportunities	Products Market share Current marketing mix Strengths and weaknesses Human resources	Competitor's sales Their profit margins Their market share Their marketing mix Their plans

2) Various **tools** are used in **analysis**, e.g. **PEST**, **SWOT** and **Cost/Benefit analysis**. There's more about these analysis tools on p.64 and 90-91, in the Objectives and Strategy section, because they're used for **more** than just marketing.

3) Various **assumptions** about **external factors** are built into the marketing plan. These include the future rate of **growth** of the **economy**, future **tax** rates, **demographics** and **competitor activities**.

Objectives and Strategies set out Marketing Aims and Directions

1) **Market objectives** say which products will be sold in which markets.

2) They can be **qualitative** (**describing** policies, brand image, product quality, product development) and **quantitative** (**specific aims** for market share, sales revenue, market penetration and profitability).

3) Marketing strategies set out the **broad plans** from which action plans and tactics are determined. They specify the **target market** and the **marketing mix**, (product, price, place and promotion).

Action Plans and Budgets give Detail of how it'll all happen

1) Action plans are detailed plans for individual marketing activities, e.g. the sales plan and the promotion plan.

2) Budgets are constructed in line with the action plans. Managers must **identify costs**, for example **advertising**, **research**, **distribution** and **personal selling** costs. Budgets are categorised by product, department or activity.

3) The whole plan has to be **monitored constantly** against specific business objectives, in order to assess performance, take corrective action, control costs and adapt the plan if it isn't working. It's important to set measurable targets for progress checking.

Practice Questions

Q1 Why is marketing called the central, integrating function?

Q2 List three factors you'd expect to see in a marketing audit.

Q3 Give examples of two qualitative and two quantitative marketing objectives.

Exam Questions

Q1 Explain the external factors that a printing business must take into account when developing its marketing plan. (6 marks)

Q2 Examine the possible benefits of marketing planning to small businesses. (8 marks)

Plans, plans, plans and more plans, nothing but plans...

The marketing plan can affect all the other functions of a business. Finance needs to make funds available to help achieve the plan, which could affect spending in other areas. HR needs to ensure there are enough staff, with the right skills, to carry out the plan. Production needs to make sure the right quantities of the right products are available at the right time.

Marketing Budget and Sales Forecasting

The marketing budget specifies the finances available for spending on marketing activities.
The sales budget uses sales forecasting to set sales targets.

A Marketing Budget is a Quantified Plan for Marketing Activities

1) Before a budget is set, the **market audit** is done — marketing managers analyse information before they set their **marketing objectives** and **strategies**. Then they come up with an **action plan** of what they're going to do, which is where the budget comes in — they need to say how much money they'll **spend** on marketing, and how much money they expect to **make** through marketing.
2) **Sales budgets** contain **sales targets** for the business in terms of volume, market share, sales growth etc.
3) **Expenditure budgets** set out the level of **spending** needed to cover the **costs** of all marketing activities — advertising, market research, distribution, personal selling etc.
4) Budgets may be categorised in terms of **products**, **departments** and **marketing activity**. Above-the-line and below-the-line activities may have separate budgets.

Expenditure Budgets can be Set in various ways

1) **Incremental budgeting** involves adding a small additional amount to the previous year's allocation, to take account of inflation. It's a very common method, because it's easy to understand and easy to do. However, it doesn't plan for unexpected events, so it can leave the firm unable to respond to new opportunities or threats.
2) **Sales-related budgeting** allocates marketing spending based on the sales revenue that the product will generate.
3) In **task-based budgeting**, marketing tasks are costed out and finances shared out accordingly.
4) **"Competitor parity" budgeting** means matching competitor spending. It's difficult to accurately determine what your competitors are spending on their marketing. They aren't likely to fax you their budget first so that you can copy it, after all. Businesses don't tend to base their budget 100% on competitors — competitor action is likely to affect the expenditure budget a bit, though.
5) The **financial state of the business** is a huge factor. Rather obviously, small businesses and new businesses are more likely to be restrained by what they can afford.

Sales Budgets depend on Past Sales, the Market, Objectives and Finances

1) **Sales targets** within sales budgets are set by looking at past figures and **extrapolating** (see next page and p.6).
2) Sales targets depend on **market conditions** — the **business cycle** and **competitor** actions can affect demand.
3) **Sales budgets** are set in line with a business's **objectives**. Priority is usually given to areas that are more likely to help the business **achieve** its objectives.
4) The **financial position** of the business and the **expenditure budget** are a factor. Spending a lot on marketing a product means that you'd expect it to **sell** pretty well.

Budget Setting has its Pitfalls

1) It's best to **consult with staff** when setting the budget. Staff **resent** not being involved in setting targets.
2) On the other hand, staff shouldn't have too much control over budget setting, because they'll set targets that are **easily reached**, or ask for more money than they need so that they won't **overspend**. Managers' **egos** are a factor as well — managers may see a large budget as an indicator of **status**.
3) Preparing budgets can be very **time consuming**, especially when there's lots of negotiation.
4) Basing an expenditure budget purely on financial position has its drawbacks. It means that the business spends a lot on marketing when sales are high, and less on marketing when sales are low — when it needs it most.
5) With **incremental budgeting**, managers may be tempted to spend the **whole budget** to make sure they get at least the same amount in next year's budget. This isn't a cost-effective way to behave.

Marketing Budgets need to be Justified by the Product

1) Budgets need to be justified in relation to the finances available, and the likely **return**. A product with a **high predicted rate of return** will earn itself a **bigger expenditure budget**.
2) **Product portfolio analysis** and the **Boston Matrix** are used to determine which products should be supported by extra spending and which "milked" to provide revenue for other marketing activities.
3) The **product life cycle** is a useful model. Marketing expenditure is likely to be high during the **launch** and **growth** phases of a product, or when **extension strategies** are being used.

Marketing Budget and Sales Forecasting

Sales Forecasting aims to Predict the Future

1) **Sales forecasting** predicts the **future sales** of a product. This allows managers to set **sales targets**. Sales performance can be measured against those targets.
2) Sales forecasts allow the **finance** department to produce **cash flow** forecasts — once they know how much the business is expected to sell, they can work out how much money is expected to come in.
3) Sales forecasts also allow **production** and **human resources** departments to gear up for the expected level of sales. They can make sure that they have the right amount of machinery, stock and staff.

Backdata and Extrapolation are Quantitative techniques for Forecasting Sales

1) **Backdata** is **data from the past**. Sales backdata from last year can be used to predict likely sales for this year. Managers look for trends in the data and **extrapolate** them forward. Moving averages and time series analysis (see p.6-7) help to identify trends in sales backdata.
2) Extrapolation is a great way of predicting sales as long as trends stay **constant**. When there's a major upheaval in the market (rare, but it does happen), extrapolation will lead you up the garden path.
3) Managers also use **market research data** to predict future sales.
4) **Test marketing** can be used to provide sales forecasts. The product is launched within a limited geographical area. Test marketing gives **accurate data**, and a **reliable** indicator of **demand**. Managers can **learn lessons** from the test marketing exercise and apply them to the full scale national launch.
5) On the other hand, test marketing allows **competitors** to look at the product before the full launch.

Qualitative Techniques such as the Delphi Method are also used

Qualitative techniques call for **human judgement**. They're particularly important when data is scarce. They include personal **insight** (hunches), **panel consensus**, and **experience** (e.g. referring to previous life cycles of similar products).

1) The **Delphi** method asks questions of a **panel of experts** in order to predict the future. The idea is that you get better prediction from human experts than from extrapolating trends.
2) The firm asks each expert **individually** for their opinion of what'll happen in the market. The experts' answers are **anonymous**. The firm puts the experts' opinions together in **summary** form, and sends the summary back to all the experts for their **comments**. The firm then summarises the comments and sends them out a second time for **further comments** and views. They repeat the process as necessary.
3) Because the original responses are **anonymous**, and each expert is asked questions **individually**, the experts won't be **swayed** by reading what the leading industry guru, or their arch-enemy, has to say.
4) The process of repeatedly summarising and asking for more comments is supposed to lead the experts towards a **consensus** view that they all agree on.

Practice Questions

Q1 List the ways budgets can be allocated.

Q2 What's the difference between sales-related budgeting and task-based budgeting?

Q3 What are the advantages of sales forecasts?

Q4 What is backdata?

Q5 What is the Delphi Method?

Exam Question

Q1 How might a company in business-to-business sales set their marketing budget? (8 marks)

Ancient weirdness ahoy...

Interesting (or perhaps not) fact — the Delphi method is named after an oracle from ancient Greek times. There was a priestess at a place called Delphi who would chew laurel leaves (poisonous, by the way) and hallucinate the answers to people's questions. Nowadays researchers ask industry big kahunas to give their opinions instead. That's progress, folks.

Company Accounts

This section builds on the Accounting and Finance section in AS Business Studies.

All businesses need Accounting Data for Decision Making

1) In order for managers to make **informed decisions** they must have access to **accurate** and **recent** financial information. They need to know **how much** their **assets** are worth, how much they **owe**, and **when** money comes in to the business or leaves the business.
2) By **law**, limited companies must produce two sets of **final accounts**. The annual **profit and loss account** (see p.16-17) details the company's performance over a year and shows money coming into the company and leaving the company. The **balance sheet** (see p.18-19) shows the company's assets and liabilities.
3) In addition, companies produce a **cash flow statement** showing the **flow of money** in and out of the business. The data is used both for planning for the future and controlling the operations of the business.
4) The law requires businesses to give information about their finances, and present their final accounts in a particular way, to make sure they're not hiding anything. This is called the **disclosure requirement**.

Stakeholders use Company Accounts to help them make decisions

1) **Managers** use all this information to make **internal** decisions.
2) **Employees** can also use the accounts to help them decide whether the business provides good career prospects.
3) The data is also used **externally** for investment decisions by existing and potential **shareholders**.
4) **Suppliers** use a firm's accounts to decide if they want to offer the firm credit — whether the firm is likely to be able to pay.
5) **Competitors** use accounts to see how a business is doing, and to figure out what the business might do next.

George and Pamela always found the company accounts a difficult balancing act.

Company Accounts must be produced according to Accounting Principles

1) All the **company's accounts must be done in the same way**. This is called the **consistency** rule, and it allows the user of the accounts to have **confidence** in the information.
2) The company accounts **assume** that the company will **keep on trading** for the **foreseeable future**.
3) Money **owed** is **"matched"** to the month of the **transaction**, not the month when the debt is paid. For example, a manufacturer sells products to a retailer in February but doesn't receive the cash for that transaction until April. The money owed to the company by the retailer is recorded in February, not April.
4) This lets the company **compare** one period of the year with another in a **fair** manner. It takes away the **coincidence** of when money is actually received — and it is a coincidence, because the debtor could just as easily have paid a month earlier or a month later.
5) Assets, liabilities or events which make "**no material difference**" to the final account can be ignored. For example, you **needn't bother** to calculate and enter a value for the seven paper clips found in the drawer when completing a stock valuation for a company with £200 000 worth of stock.
6) **Accounts must be based on fact, not opinion.** This rule is to avoid **falsehood** and **bias** in producing final accounts. Assets must be listed as what they're really worth, not what you'd like them to be worth.
7) Assets are valued as their value to the business **right now**, not their purchase price when **new**.
8) If in doubt, company accounts should overstate losses and understate profits. By overstating losses and understating profits, you'll **never** end up with **less** money than you expect, and you might well end up with **more** money than you expect. This rule is designed to balance out the tendency of managers to be **over-optimistic** — e.g. they may overstate the ability of a customer to pay.

Company Accounts

Revenue Expenditure and Capital Expenditure are Different

Expenditure is a fancy way of saying "spending".

1) Expenditure is classified according to whether it **adds value to the business as a whole**, or whether it's a **necessary expenditure of doing business**.
2) **Capital expenditure** is money used to buy **fixed assets**. These are things used over and over again to produce goods or services for sale — e.g. **factories** and **equipment**. Businesses need capital expenditure to **start up**, to **expand** and to **replace** worn out equipment.
3) **Fixed assets** can be **sold**, so capital expenditure doesn't represent money that's lost and gone forever. Fixed assets are used to produce things for sale, to make surplus revenue — they **make more money** for the business.
4) **Revenue expenditure** (**or working capital**) is the cash needed to pay for the **daily running** of a business. It's used to pay wages, suppliers, electricity/gas bills, business rates etc.
5) **Revenue expenditure** does represent money that's **gone for good**. Once you've paid the tax man or the electricity provider, that's it.
6) **Capital expenditure** allows a business to **grow**. **Revenue expenditure** allows a business to **survive**. All businesses need **both** types of finance.

You can find Revenue Expenditure and Capital Expenditure on the Accounts

1) You'll find **capital expenditure** on the balance sheet, in the form of **fixed assets**, and the **capital** used to purchase them. See p.18-19 for more about the balance sheet.
2) You'll find **working capital** (**revenue expenditure**) on the profit and loss account, in the form of **expenses**. See p.16-17 for more about the profit and loss account.
3) You can also work out **working capital** from the **balance sheet**. Working capital is the difference between **current assets** and **current liabilities**. **Current assets** are things that the business can **quickly turn into cash**, e.g. stocks of finished goods, or debts owed by customers. **Current liabilities** are debts that the business will have to **repay** within the year, e.g. money owed to suppliers.

   Working capital = current assets – current liabilities

4) The amount of working capital is predicted using the **cash flow forecast**.

Dishonest firms try to confuse Revenue Expenditure and Capital Expenditure

1) **Capital expenditure** is in general a **good** and **lovely thing**. It represents **investment** in the firm — **fixed assets** which can be used to **generate profit**, and sold on to generate cash if needed.
2) **Revenue expenditure** is a **necessary evil**. It represents expenses. It's a loss on the profit and loss account.
3) Dishonest firms sometimes **pretend** that money they've spent as **revenue expenditure** was spent on fixed assets as **capital expenditure** instead, to make it look like they've got more to show for the money they've spent. This is a form of window-dressing — see p.23 for why firms do this.

Practice Questions

Q1 Why do companies keep accounts?

Q2 Why must all a company's accounts be done in the same way?

Q3 What is revenue expenditure?

Q4 What is capital expenditure?

Exam Question

Q1 Why is it harmful to stakeholders to falsely classify revenue expenditure as capital expenditure? (10 marks)

Ah yes, but there's no accounting for taste...

Most of this builds on the AS Accounting and Finance section. Here, the same content is covered, but in plenty more detail, and there's some brand new content too. Learn the accounting principles and why they exist — the underlying idea of all the principles and the disclosure requirement is that firms shouldn't be able to hide the truth about their financial affairs.

Company Accounts: Profit and Loss

The profit and loss account is a very useful collection of financial information.

Profit and Loss Accounts show Revenue and Expenses

1) The profit and loss account show how much money's been **coming into the company** (**revenue**) and how much has been **going out** (**expenses**).
2) Revenue is **sales income** from selling goods and services. This includes **cash payments** received and sales on **credit**.
3) Expenses are all the **costs** of the business. These are divided into **direct** and **indirect** costs, or **fixed** and **variable** costs.
4) Profit and loss accounts show revenue expenditure, and balance sheets show capital expenditure.

Remember that accounting follows the matching principle — sales income is recorded when the sale's made, not when the customer pays.

Profit = Revenue – Expenses (and there are different categories of profit...)

1) **Gross profit** is **revenue** minus **direct costs**. The direct cost of making and selling a product include raw materials and wages of production workers, but not wages of other staff. These direct costs are called the **cost of sales** on the profit and loss account.
2) **Net profit** is **gross profit** minus **indirect costs**. Indirect costs (**overheads**) cover wages of non-production staff, advertising, office rent, rates, interest payments and depreciation (see p.21).
3) **Operating profit** takes into account all revenues and costs from **regular trading**, but not any revenues and costs from **one-off** events. It only covers activities that are likely to be **repeated year on year**.
4) **Net profit before tax** covers **all revenues and costs**, including those from **one-off events** such as the sale or purchase of another business.
5) **Net profit after tax** is what's left after corporation tax has been paid.
6) **Retained profit** is what's left from net profit after tax, once **share dividends** have been paid to shareholders.

Maud was mainly interested in net profit.

One-off profit is Low Quality — Sustained profit is High Quality

1) Profit can be "**high quality**" or "**low quality**", depending on whether it's likely to carry on into the future.
2) Profit from **one-off events** like the sale of part of the business is considered to be **low quality**.
3) **Operating profit** is **high quality**, because it's probably going to carry on being made year on year.
4) **Shareholders** like **high quality** profit, because they want profit to continue into the future. Future profits mean future dividend payments and happy shareholders.

The Profit and Loss Account is Three accounts in One

1) The **trading account** works out **gross profit** — revenue minus direct costs.
2) The **profit and loss account** subtracts overheads (indirect costs) to work out **operating profit** and **net profit**.
3) The **appropriation account** shows what's done with profits — it's either **distributed** between shareholders, or **kept** in the business to invest in future activities. The appropriation account works out **retained profit**.

Profit and Loss Accounts calculate Profits over a period of Time

Profit and loss accounts should cover one whole accounting year. A profit and loss account that covers **less than 12 months** can be **misleading**. High Street retailers can generate **half their annual revenue** in the lead-up to **Christmas** — a profit and loss account ignoring this period won't give anything like an accurate picture of the business.

Sometimes profit and loss accounts cover a little **more** or a little **less** than a year — e.g. when a business changes its accounting year from Dec-Dec to Apr-Apr, it'll have one set of accounts that cover Dec-Apr.

Profit and loss accounts usually contain the **previous year's data** as well, for **easy comparison** to see what's changed. Some companies provide the previous five years' data as well. It's very useful to be able to spot trends in turnover, costs and profits.

Company Accounts: Profit and Loss

Here's a **Reminder** of what the **Profit and Loss Account** looks like

ABC Company Ltd
Profit and Loss Account for the year ended 30 March 2004

The title includes the period covered by the account.

This subtracts direct costs (cost of sales) from revenue generated to get gross profit.

Trading Account	Revenue		£100 000
	Opening stock	£3000	
	Purchases	£42 000	
	Closing Stock	(£5000)	
	Cost of sales		(£40 000)
	Gross Profit		**£60 000**
Profit and loss Account	Wages	£15 000	
	Rent	£8000	
	Advertising	£12 000	
	Depreciation	£5000	
	Total overheads		(£40 000)
	Net Profit		**£20 000**
Appropriation Account	Tax		(£5000)
	Dividends		(£7000)
	Retained profit		**£8000**
	Earnings per share		**£5.80p**
	Dividend per share		**£2.70p**

Revenue only includes completed sales, where the goods are delivered to the customer. It makes no difference when the payment is received.

Cost of sales = purchases + (opening stock – closing stock). Cost of sales only relates to sales made during this trading period. The cost of producing stock still in the warehouse doesn't count.

Gross profit = revenue – cost of sales

This shows expenses, and subtracts expenses from gross profit to get net profit.

Depreciation is the annual drop in value of assets as they get older (see p.21).

Net profit = gross profit – overheads

This classifies profit according to what it's used for. Profit utilisation is the technical term for how a business uses its profit after tax.

Amount paid out to shareholders.

Retained profit = net profit – (tax + dividends)

Profit after tax ÷ number of shares

Total dividends ÷ number of shares

Stakeholders have an **Interest** in the **Profit and Loss Account**

1) **Managers** use the profit and loss account to judge **business performance**. They're interested in the **cost of sales** compared with **sales revenue** — this shouldn't be too high. They're also interested in how much profit was from **one-off items** — they prefer the profit to be high quality.
2) **Employees** are interested in how much **profit** the business is making, as an indicator of **job security** and potential **pay rises**. They'll be especially interested in profits if there's a **profit-related** link in their pay scheme.
3) Shareholders want to know the company's **turnover**, and the **operating profit**, so that they can see how the company is **performing** compared to previous years.
4) Shareholders also like to check **profit appropriation**. Some shareholders like to get as much **dividend** as possible for a short-term return. Some prefer to see money being **reinvested** into the business for long-term returns.
5) Limited companies and partnerships with a turnover over £15 million have to submit their accounts to the **Inland Revenue**. The tax man is interested in **net profit** before tax, because that's what a business is **taxed** on. The Inland Revenue also check through the accounts to make sure that the accounts procedure is up to standard.

Practice Questions

Q1 What is operating profit?

Q2 What is retained profit?

Q3 Define high quality profit.

Q4 Which parts of the profit and loss account are shareholders most interested in?

Exam Question

Q1 Discuss whether the profit and loss account gives a good indication of the financial wellbeing of a business. (12 marks)

Step 1: buy stuff. Step 2: sell stuff. Step 3: PROFIT...

Well, that's the simplest way of looking at business, I suppose. What the examiners expect you to know about profit for this section is not so much how it's made, but what kind of profit it is. Profit can be gross, net, retained, operating, low quality or high quality. If you don't know what one or other of those terms mean, you need to revise these pages again.

Company Accounts: Balance Sheets

You've come across balance sheets at AS level, but there's considerably more detail and depth for A2 level, so learn it all.

Balance Sheets are lists of Assets and Liabilities

1) Balance sheets are a **snapshot** of a firm's finances at a **fixed point in time**. They show the value of all the **assets** (the things that belong to the business, including cash in the bank) and all the **liabilities** (the money the business owes). They also show the value of all the **capital** in the business, and the source of that capital — they show where the money's **come from** as well as what's being **done** with it.
2) The **value** of the **assets** purchased **equals** the **amount of money** used to **buy** them. Balance sheets... **balance**.

Assets are things the Business Owns (that it's bought with capital)

1) Assets includes **machinery**, **stock**, **property**, **land**, and **cash**, as well as money owed to the business by **debtors**.
2) Assets can be classified as **fixed assets** or **current assets** — see the table below.

Fixed assets	Current assets
These are kept for **more than a year** — e.g. property, land, production equipment, desks and computers. Fixed assets **depreciate** — see p.21.	These are likely to be exchanged for cash **within the accounting year**, before the next balance sheet is worked out. **Stock** and **debtors** are current assets.

3) Assets can also be classified as **tangible** or **intangible**.

- **Tangible assets** are **actual physical stuff** such as property, stock or machinery.
- **Intangible assets** are **non-physical things** like brands, customer goodwill, patents and licenses. It's easy to include them on the balance sheet if they have an **objective**, **quantifiable** value — if a **definite amount of money** was spent on them. For example, 3G mobile phone **licences** were bought from the government for an amount of **money**, which can go on the balance sheet. But the **brand** of a particular mobile phone company such as 3 or Vodafone can't be easily quantified. See p.23 for more on intangible assets.

4) **Ideally**, every debt owed by debtors to the business would be paid. **Unfortunately**, the **real world** isn't like that. Debts which don't get paid are called "**bad debts**". These bad debts **can't** be included on the balance sheet as an **asset** — because the business isn't going to get money for them.
5) The business **writes off** bad debts, and puts them as an **expense** on the profit and loss account.

Liabilities are Debts the Business Owes (where its capital has come from)

1) **Current liabilities** are **debts** which need to be paid off within a year. They include overdrafts, taxes due to be paid, money owed to creditors and dividends due to be paid to shareholders.
2) **Long term liabilities** are debts that the business will pay off over several years, e.g. mortgages and loans.
3) All the company's **sources of capital** count as a liability, even money invested by **shareholders**. This is because if the business ceased trading, the shareholders would want their money back. The owner's equity (money they've put in) counts as a liability for a **partnership** as well.
4) **Reserves** are mostly retained profits, and also include money from any rises in asset value. Reserves count as a **liability** because they're a **source of finance**.

Liabilities = where the money's from.
Assets = what you've done with it.

Balance Sheets show the Short Term Financial Status of the Company

1) The balance sheet shows you how much the business is **worth**.
2) **Working capital** (net current assets) is the amount of money the business has available in the short term. It's calculated by subtracting **current liabilities** from **current assets**. See p.22 for more on working capital.
3) **Suppliers** are particularly interested in **working capital** and **liquidity**. Suppliers can look at the balance sheet to see how liquid the firm's assets are, as well as how much working capital the firm has. The more liquid the assets, the better the firm will be at paying bills. This helps them decide whether to offer the business supplies on **credit**, and how much credit to offer.

Liquidity = how easy it is to pay debt. See p.22. The liquidity of an asset is how easy it is to turn it into cash and spend it. Cash is the most liquid asset, then debtors, stock and short term investments.

4) The balance sheet shows **sources of capital**. Ideally, **long-term loans** or **mortgages** are used to finance the purchase of fixed assets. A well managed business wouldn't borrow too much through **short-term overdrafts**, because overdrafts are an expensive way of borrowing.

Company Accounts: Balance Sheets

Interpreting balance sheets — Here's How It All Looks

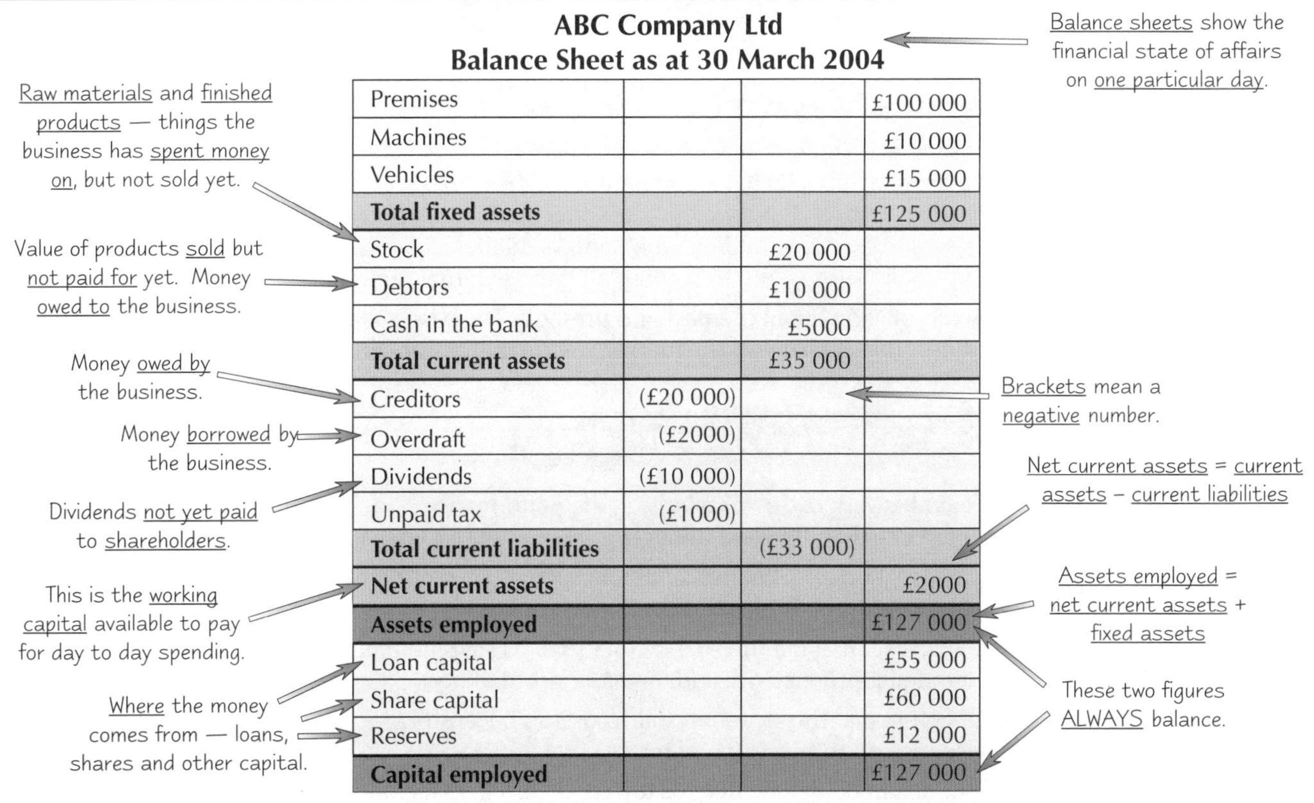

ABC Company Ltd
Balance Sheet as at 30 March 2004

Premises			£100 000
Machines			£10 000
Vehicles			£15 000
Total fixed assets			£125 000
Stock		£20 000	
Debtors		£10 000	
Cash in the bank		£5000	
Total current assets		£35 000	
Creditors	(£20 000)		
Overdraft	(£2000)		
Dividends	(£10 000)		
Unpaid tax	(£1000)		
Total current liabilities		(£33 000)	
Net current assets			£2000
Assets employed			£127 000
Loan capital			£55 000
Share capital			£60 000
Reserves			£12 000
Capital employed			£127 000

*By **Comparing Balance Sheets** you can see **Long-Term Trends***

1) Comparing this year's balance sheet to previous years' accounts lets you pick out **trends** in company finances. Looking at the "bottom line" over several years shows you how the business is **growing**.
2) A **quick increase** in **fixed assets** indicates that the company has invested in property or machinery. This means that the company is investing in a growth strategy, and may make more profit over the medium term — useful information for shareholders and potential shareholders, who want to see more profit.
3) Increases in **reserves** also suggest an increase in **profits** — good news for shareholders.
4) The balance sheet shows **trends** in how the business has **raised its capital**. It's risky to suddenly start borrowing a lot, in case interest rates rise. A company with a high value of creditors and a relatively low value of share capital or reserves would be in trouble if the Bank of England put interest rates up.

Practice Questions

Q1 Give two examples of fixed assets, and two examples of current assets.
Q2 Give an example of an intangible asset.
Q3 What are bad debts?
Q4 Why is share capital classified as a liability?

Exam Question

Q1 The balance sheet of Joanne's hairdressing salon shows fixed assets of £4000, £400 stock, £50 debtors, £150 cash, and current liabilities of £120. The business has £3000 from a long term business loan and reserves of £1480. Evaluate the current position of Joanne's business. (12 marks)

Liabilities = where the money's from. Assets = what the money's paid for...

Balance sheets can seem weird — why are reserves liabilities when cash is an asset, for example. If you see it as where the money's from, and what the firm's done with it, you can see what goes where and why it balances. Examiners love this stuff. Make sure you look carefully at what managers and stakeholders can actually learn from the balance sheet.

Limitations of Accounts

Accounts are useful, but they aren't the be-all and end-all of financial health.

Accounts Don't Contain anything Non-Numerical

1) **Internal strengths** such as the quality of staff, or the company's market share, don't appear on the accounts. You'd need to do a **SWOT** analysis (see p.90) to find them out.
2) **External factors** such as the **economic** or **market** environment aren't reflected in the accounts. Accounts don't tell you anything about what a **competitor** might do next, or what legislation might be passed by the government. The development of **technology**, or potential changes to the **location** of the business (e.g. a new rail link) don't appear in the accounts. You'd need to do a **PEST** analysis (see p.90) to sort out all these **external factors**.
3) Accounts only contain information about the **past** and **present**. The past isn't always a good guide to the future. Things **change**. The market environment is **uncertain**.

The Profit and Loss Account doesn't Tell All

1) The **profit and loss account** is very useful for assessing the performance of the company. It isn't the be-all and end-all, though.
2) It doesn't include any information about **external factors** such as **market demand**, which would be useful in forecasting **future turnover** and **profit**.
3) It doesn't include any information about **internal factors** such as staff morale, which would be useful in determining **productivity** and therefore **profitability**.
4) In times of **inflation**, the profit and loss account isn't so useful, because inflationary rises in price distort the true value of turnover.
5) The profit and loss account can be **deliberately distorted**, by bringing forward sales from the next trading period and including them as part of this trading period.
6) The profit and loss account can also be **window-dressed** by depreciating assets too slowly and by capitalising expenditure (see p.23).

The Balance Sheet Doesn't Tell All, either

1) The **balance sheet** is a statement about one point in the **past**, which may not help predict the **future**.
2) The balance sheet doesn't give any clues about the **market** or the **economy** that the business is trading in.
3) Balance sheets value some intangible assets (e.g. a brand recently purchased by the company), but they don't value intangible assets like **staff skill**, **staff motivation** or **management experience**.

Bad Debts are Subjective — it's not wise to be too Optimistic or too Cautious

1) Remember, **bad debts** are debts owed to a business that the **debtor won't ever pay**. Debts owed to a business that will be paid go on the balance sheet as an asset. Bad debts go on the profit and loss account as an expense.
2) It's important to be **realistic** about bad debts. The business shouldn't be **over optimistic** and report debts as **assets** when it's unlikely that they're ever going to be paid. On the other hand, they shouldn't be **too cautious** and write debts off as **bad debts** when they could make the debtors pay up.

- Being **overoptimistic** results in an asset valuation that's **too high**.
- Being **over cautious** results in an asset valuation that's **too low**.

It's best to look at the Profit and Loss Account together with the Balance Sheet

The profit and loss account and balance sheet are much stronger taken **together** than separately.

The **Directors' Report** gives more information than either, but it isn't available **outside** the company.

Depreciation

Most assets lose value over time. This is called depreciation.

Accounts reflect **Assets** that **Depreciate** — they **Lose Value** over **Time**

1) The **drop in value** of a business asset over time is called **depreciation**. Assets lose value for three main reasons. They suffer **wear and tear**, they need **expensive repairs**, and they become **old fashioned** compared to newer kit.
2) Businesses **calculate depreciation** each year to make sure that an asset's **value** on the **balance sheet** is a **true reflection** of what the business would get from **selling** it.
3) Building depreciation into each year's accounts **stops** it hitting **all at once** when the business **sells** the asset. By depreciating a piece of machinery over 10 years, a business can take a tenth of the cost of the equipment into account each year. Without depreciating the asset, the business would be **understating their costs** (therefore overstating their profits) for each year until they got rid of the asset at which point they'd suddenly be massively overstating their costs. Spreading out the cost allows the business to make comparisons between financial years.
4) The **amount lost** through depreciation is recorded on the **profit and loss account** as an **expense**. It's unusual in that it isn't a cash expense. It's a recognition of the money that's been sunk into the asset that can't ever be got back. Depreciation is a form of **revenue expenditure**.

Use the **Straight Line** method to calculate **Depreciation**

1) The **straight line method** of calculating depreciation splits it equally over the life of an asset.
2) This method is quick and simple, but you need to know how long the asset **lasts** and how much it's worth when you eventually replace it. The amount an asset is worth when you get rid of it is called its **residual value**.
3) The straight line method **isn't perfect**. In reality, assets often **lose more value early on** in their life, rather than losing value **steadily** over a period of time.

$$\text{Depreciation per year} = \frac{\text{cost of asset} - \text{residual value}}{\text{useful life of asset}}$$

Example: A piece of machinery costs **£10 000** when new. It's expected to last **8 years**. After 8 years, it's worth **£500**.

$$\text{Depreciation} = \frac{£10\,000 - £500}{8} = £1187.50$$

Working out **Depreciation** can be partly **Subjective**

1) There's a **subjective** side to working out depreciation — figuring out how long an asset will last requires some subjective **human judgement**.
2) An asset that's well looked after won't depreciate as fast as one that's knocked about.

Practice Questions

Q1 Other than the balance sheet, describe two sources of data that would tell you about a firm's financial health.

Q2 From the point of view of asset valuation, why is it important not to be too cautious about bad debts?

Q3 Is depreciation capital expenditure or revenue expenditure?

Q4 What is meant by "residual value"?

Exam Question

Q1 Analyse the value of a balance sheet to an investor considering buying shares in a football club. (12 marks)

Q2 Rob Williams has just bought a new computer system for his office, at a cost of £2500. He intends to replace it after 4 years, when he calculates he'll be able to sell it for £500. How much should he depreciate the asset value of the computer system by this year? (6 marks)

Answer on p.98.

On balance it's more than likely to come up in the exam...

Examiners like to ask you what the limitations of the published accounts are. You also need to learn about depreciation. This includes knowing what it is, why it's done and where it's recorded. You also have to learn how to do depreciation calculations. Luckily, they're not really that hard.

Working Capital

Working capital is the money available to fund day-to-day expenditure. Managers must regularly plan, control and review the use of this money (cash, stock and debtors).

Businesses **Need Enough Working Capital** but not too much

Working capital = **current assets** (cash, debtors and stock) – **current liabilities** (overdraft, creditors, tax)

Businesses need working capital for liquidity — **liquidity** is a measure of the company's ability to **pay its debt**. In addition to generating sales the business needs to **collect money** as quickly as possible from customers, so that it has enough **working capital** to pay its liabilities. See p.24, 'Financial Ratios', for liquidity ratios.

Businesses need **just enough** working capital to pay short term debts. They shouldn't have too much working capital. **Liquid assets** like cash and debtors are great at **paying off debts**, but lousy at **earning money** for the business. To make money, the business needs **fixed assets** that work hard and make sales possible.

Factors affecting how much working capital a business needs:

1) Businesses with **high sales volume** tend to have high cost of sales, so they need more working capital.
2) The more **credit** a business offers, the more **working capital** it needs to fend off a **cash flow crisis.**
3) The longer the **cash flow cycle/operating cycle**, the more working capital is needed. E.g. supermarkets have a short operating cycle because they don't hold stocks for long, and they don't have to wait for payment on credit. 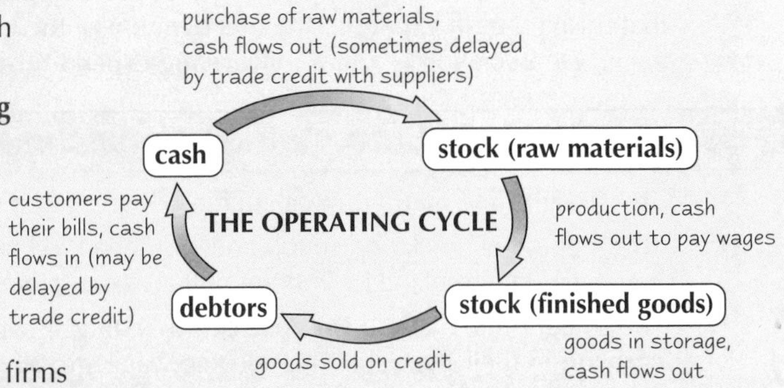
4) **Inflation** increases the costs of wages and stock, so firms need more working capital in times when inflation is high.
5) When a business **expands**, it needs more working capital to avoid **overtrading**. Overtrading means producing so much that the business can't pay its suppliers before it gets the chance to be paid by its customers.

Businesses must **Control** their **Debtors**

1) A business needs to control its **debtors** (people who owe money to the firm).
2) A company which has sold millions of pounds worth of goods over, say, a three-month period but hasn't made sure that **payment** has been received will have **no money coming in**.
3) Wages, tax, loan repayments and interest must still be paid, so it's very important to control debtors in order to remain in a position of **liquidity**. (See p.32, cash flow forecasting).

Businesses must **Control** their **Stock**

1) A business needs to control the volume of its **stock** (raw materials and unsold products) to get a level that allows the business to satisfy the demands of the market.
2) A business that holds **too little stock** will **lose sales** because it won't be able to supply enough goods to the market.
3) A business that holds **too much stock** has money in the form of stock which isn't able to **work** for the company elsewhere. Money tied up in stock could either be helping improve liquidity by paying debt and wages, or helping improve productivity by being invested in new projects.

Stock is **Valued** at **Cost** or at **Net Realisable Value**, whichever's **Lower**

1) Accounting conventions say that stock values on the balance sheet must be **realisable**. This means that the stock value must be the price which you'd actually get if you sold the stock right now in its present state.
2) This realisable price could well be **less** than the **original cost** that the business paid for the stock.
3) The rules are that the company must record the stock value as being the **lower** value of **cost** and **net realisable value**.
4) To put this into context, say a business buys **300 microprocessors** at **£30 000** (cost of £100 each) for the production of its laptop computers. Later, it **updates** the specification of the laptops and has to sell the microprocessors. In the mean time, technological advances mean that there are new, faster microchips on the market. There's little demand for the old microprocessors, and the firm can only sell the old stock for £40 each (£12 000 for the lot). The **lower value** for the stock (£12 000 rather than £30 000) is recorded in the accounts.

Window Dressing

*The apparent strength of the final published accounts can be **legally manipulated** in various ways. This is called window dressing.*

It's Easy to Inflate the Value of Brands and other Intangible Assets

1) Customers may make purchase decisions based upon a brand name. This means the **brand name** has a **value**, especially if the company is ever for sale. It's an asset of the company, but it is **intangible** — it can't be picked up or touched. Other intangible assets include **goodwill**, **patents**, **copyrights** and **trademarks** — non-physical possessions of the company which help the company make money.
2) Brands which have been **recently acquired** for **money** have to go on the balance sheet. Brands which have been in the company for a while **don't** go on the balance sheet. This is because the board of directors would decide on the valuation of these internal brands — and it would be far too easy to make up outrageous valuations.
3) Brands that have been **acquired** for money can **still** be **over-valued** by the business, by the simple tactic of not **depreciating** them enough. This is perfectly legal, if technically somewhat naughty.

Sale and Leaseback is open to Manipulation

1) A company may decide to **sell** its fleet of vehicles to a leasing company and then **lease** (similar to renting) the vehicles back for an agreed period of time.
2) The leasing company gains a customer and the company benefits from having a **lump sum payment** for the value of the assets sold to the leasing company.
3) This lump payment is an **income** for the company and it'll appear on the **profit and loss account** — so the **profit** will show an **increase**. This is great news if the natural level of profit is insufficient to meet company **objectives**.
4) There'll be **reduced fixed assets** on the balance sheet and more liquid cash, so hey presto, the **liquidity** position of the company is altered.
5) This method can't be applied every year — once you've sold some assets and leased them back you can't do the same thing to the same assets the next year.

"Now let us draw the curtains of sale and leaseback and close the shutters of overvalued brand assets..."

Businesses can "Capitalise Expenditure" — count Expenses as Fixed Assets

Businesses sometimes play tricks by classifying **revenue expenditure** (which is an **expense** on the profit and loss account) as **capital expenditure** (a **fixed asset** on the balance sheet). Balance sheet assets look good, and can be **depreciated over several years**, which is nicer than having the expenditure hitting the profit and loss account all at once.

See p.15 for more about capital expenditure and revenue expenditure.

Investors and **suppliers** use the final accounts to make **judgements** regarding a company, so it's important that these people are **aware** of the methods that can be used to enhance the final figures.

Practice Questions

Q1 Why is it important to have (a) enough working capital (b) not too much working capital?

Q2 What does the term "intangible asset" mean?

Q3 What is sale and leaseback?

Q4 How does sale and leaseback affect the profit and loss account?

Exam Questions

Q1 Describe one method available to a company to affect the apparent strength of the published accounts. (6 marks)

Q2 Discuss the effect of intangible asset valuation on the liquidity of a company. (8 marks)

Trust me, I'm a Director...

To be honest, these are two separate topics, but they're both needed for the exam, and they're both related to how the profit and loss account and balance sheet are used. Businesses use all sorts of tricks to make it look as if they have more in assets than they really have, or to make it look like they're making smaller losses and bigger profits than they really are.

Financial Ratios

Ratio analysis turns final accounts into easy to understand numbers. You can use ratios to compare firms and to compare the performance of a firm from one year to the next.

Liquidity Ratios show How Much Money is available to Pay The Bills

1) A firm without enough **working capital** is suffering from poor **liquidity**. It has the assets, but it can't **use** them to **pay** for things here and now.
2) The **liquidity** of an asset is how easily it can be turned into **cash** and used to **buy** things. **Cash** is **very** liquid, **fixed assets** such as **factories** are **not liquid**, stocks and money owed by debtors are in between.
3) A business which doesn't have enough current assets to pay their liabilities when they are due is **insolvent**. They either have to quickly find the money to pay them, give up and **cease trading**, or go bankrupt.
4) **Working capital** and **liquidity** can be **improved** by decreasing stocks, introducing just-in-time production methods, speeding up collection of debts owed to the business, or slowing down payments to creditors (e.g. suppliers).

The Acid Test Ratio is the only Liquidity Ratio you need to know

1) The **acid test ratio** compares **current assets (excluding stock)** to current liabilities. It shows how much of what a business owes in the short-term is covered by its current assets. It doesn't include stock, because it isn't always easy to sell stock in time to pay off debts.

$$\textbf{Acid test ratio} = \frac{\textbf{Current assets – Stock}}{\textbf{Current liabilities}} \quad \text{(written as a ratio } x\text{:}1\text{)}$$

For example: $\frac{£30\,000}{£32\,000} = 0.9375:1$

2) A ratio of 1:1 is ideal — it shows **both** amounts are the **same**, so a business can afford to pay off all its immediately debts without having to rely on its stock.
3) A value much **more** than this, e.g. 1.5:1, means the business has **money lying around** that they could use more profitably if they invested it elsewhere.
4) A ratio of less than 1:1 means the business doesn't have **enough** current assets to **pay its bills.** A ratio of 0.8:1 shows a firm has only 80p of liquid assets for every £1 of current liabilities it owes. Not good...

When using liquidity ratios, managers have to be careful that a poor ratio doesn't turn into a **self-fulfilling prophecy**. For example, an acid test ratio of 0.8:1 suggests a liquidity problem. A manager might **overreact** to the problem and get the business in even more trouble. This kind of self-fulfilling prophecy is called **determinism**.

Efficiency or Performance ratios show how Efficiently the business is working

Efficiency ratios show how efficiently the business is using its **resources**. It's generally a good idea for a business to be getting as much **turnover** from its **assets** as possible. It's also generally a good idea to not have too much assets as **stock** or as **debtors**.

1) Asset Turnover Ratio = Sales Revenue ÷ Assets x 100

$$\textbf{Asset Turnover ratio} = \frac{\textbf{Sales Revenue}}{\textbf{Assets}} \times 100$$

1) **Fixed assets** are things like **machinery** which help the business operate efficiently, and so make lots of sales (turnover).
2) What counts as a **good** asset turnover ratio depends on the type of business. A **discount** retailer makes a lot of sales and has low value stock, so it'd have a **high asset turnover** ratio. A **luxury** retailer such as a Rolls Royce showroom makes fewer sales, and has higher value stock, so it'd have a **lower asset turnover** ratio.
3) Managers should **compare** the asset turnover ratio to **previous operating periods**, to see if the firm is **improving** its efficiency month after month, or year after year.
4) The asset turnover ratio can be **improved** by making sure that the firm **sells everything** it makes.
5) Operating machinery to **full capacity** helps get the most sales out of your fixed assets. There are **problems** with this — machinery operating at its limit may break down and need **expensive** repair or **very expensive** replacement. It's better to simply **get rid** of under-used fixed assets.

Financial Ratios

2) *Stock Turnover Ratio* = *Cost of Sales (per year) ÷ Average Stock Held*

$$\text{Stock Turnover} = \frac{\text{Cost of Sales}}{\text{Average Stock Held}}$$

You need to know the value of sales AT COST, i.e. what they cost the business to make. Stock is valued at cost price, so you need sales at cost price too. You'll find cost of sales on the profit and loss account, and stock held is on the balance sheet.

1) This ratio tells you **how many times** a year the business **sells all its stock**.
   - A fruit and veg stall which opened **6 days a week** might sell their **entire stock every day**, which would give a stock turnover ratio of **312** (6 days a week times 52 weeks a year).
   - A property developer who took **4 months to do up and sell each house** would have a stock turnover ratio of **3** (because they'd sell 3 houses in every 12 months).
   - Businesses operating **JIT production** have a **very high** ratio, because they keep the bare minimum of stock, and re-order stock all the time.
2) When you analyse this ratio, you need to judge if the business has **enough stock** to **fulfil orders**, but **not so much stock** that they're **inefficient**. Holding twice the stock needed might not be an efficient use of funds. You also need to remember that typical ratios will vary between different industries.
3) The **higher** the stock turnover is the **better** — it means that money isn't tied up in stock for long periods of time. It also means that a business should be more **competitive** as it gets to make a profit on its stock quicker.
4) A **low stock turnover** means that a business has **slow moving stock**.
5) The ratio can be improved by **holding less stock**, using **better stock control methods** like just-in-time production, or by **increasing sales**. The disadvantages of implementing any of these actions could include the expense of introducing new stock control procedures and not being able to respond to unexpected increases in demand.
6) **Aged stock analysis** lets managers make sure that old stock gets sold before it becomes **obsolete** and **unsaleable**. It lists all stock in **age order**, so the manager can **discount** old stock and cut down orders for slow selling stock.

3) *Debtor Days Ratio* = *Average Debtors ÷ Total Credit Sales × 365*

$$\text{Debtor Days} = \frac{\text{Average Debtors}}{\text{Total Credit Sales}} \times 365$$

You'll find "debtors" on the balance sheet as a current asset — it's the amount of money owed to the firm by all its debtors. You can average over two years' balance sheets to get the average debtors over the trading period.

1) Debtor Days is the number of days that the business has to **wait to be paid** for goods it supplies on credit.
2) It's best to have **low** debtor days, because it helps with **cash flow** and **working capital**. What makes a good debtor days ratio depends on the type of business. **Retailers** tend to get paid **straight away** unless they're offering credit on items such as TVs or fridges. **Medium size businesses** usually take **70-90 days** to get invoices paid.
3) You can **compare** debtor days ratios with previous months or years to look for **trends**. An **upward trend** may be because the business has offered **longer credit terms** to attract more customers. However, if it isn't monitored, the business may be heading for **cash flow problems**.
4) The debtor days ratio can be **improved** by **debt factoring** or by introducing new **policies** to reduce the likeliness of bad debts. However, customers might not like it, and in extreme instances could take their business elsewhere.
5) **Aged debtors analysis** lets managers **control debtor days**. Unpaid accounts are listed in order of how long they've been unpaid. The ones that are **most overdue** are **targeted** first for repayment.

Practice Questions

Q1 A firm has £40 000 assets, £10 000 of which is stock, and £28 000 liabilities. Work out the acid test ratio.

Q2 Which would have the higher stock turnover ratio, a Porsche dealer or a shoe shop?

Exam Questions

Q1 Comment on the efficiency of a firm that this year has revenue of £750 000 using £2 000 000 in assets. The previous year the firm had an asset turnover ratio of 25%. Has their asset turnover improved? (6 marks)

Oh look, what a lot of "lovely" ratios...

Being totally honest, these ratios are a right pain in the backside to learn. There are a lot of them, and they're practically all something divided by something else, which makes them easy to mix up. Knowing these ratios can score you good marks, so take the time to learn each one, and make sure you know what the answers of the ratios mean for the business.

Financial Ratios: Investment

Investment ratios show the risk of investing in a business.
There's always some risk — you might not get your money back.

Gearing shows **Where** a business gets its **Capital** from

1) **Gearing** shows the **percentage** of a business's capital that comes from **long-term loans** (debt) rather than **share capital** or **reserves** (equity).

$$\text{Gearing} = \frac{\text{Long-term loans}}{\text{Capital employed}} \times 100\ \%$$

2) A gearing **above 50%** shows a business is **high-geared**, **below 50%** shows it is **low-geared**.

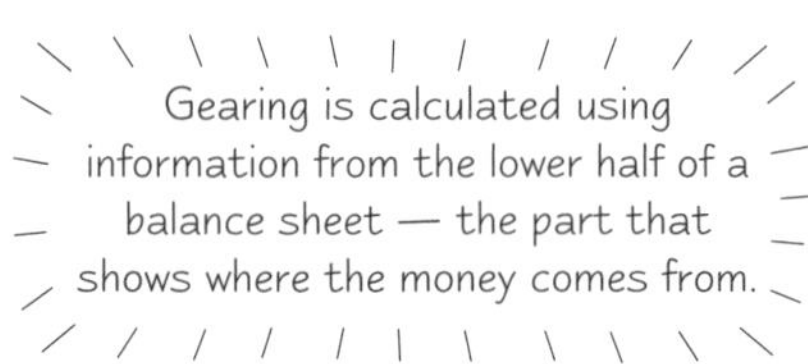

Gearing shows how **Vulnerable** a business is to **Changes** in **Interest Rates**

1) The more the business is **borrowing**, the harder they'll be hit by a rise in interest rates.
2) This is a crude **risk assessment** that an investor can use to help them decide whether to buy shares in the company. The more the firm borrows, the **more interest** it will have to pay — and this may affect **profits** and the **dividend** paid to shareholders. The more the firm borrows, the more **risk** there is that the investor won't get much dividend.

Example: A firm has gearing of 11% — it's low geared.
- This tells you that **most** long-term funds come from **shareholders**, not loans.
- You can tell that the firm is **risk averse** — it doesn't want to run the risk of spending too much money on interest payments.
- Because the firm doesn't have to spend its profits on interest payments, it can withstand a fall in profits more easily than a highly geared firm.

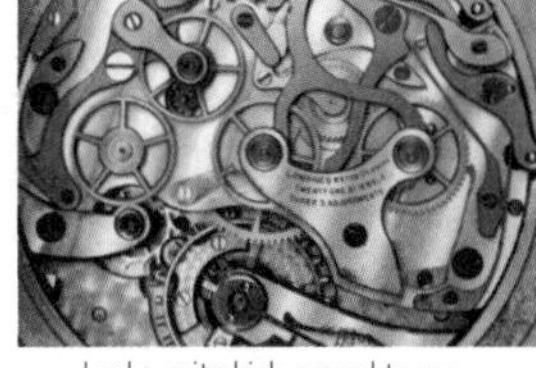
Looks quite high geared to me...

High Gearing has **Risks** and **Rewards** — for both **Businesses** and **Investors**

1) The **reward** of **borrowing** money for the business is extra **funds** for expansion. Ideally, the loan is invested in projects or technology, which **increase profits** by more than enough to pay off the loan repayments.
2) The **risk** to the business of **borrowing** money is that it might not be able to afford the repayments — it might not make enough profit to pay back the loan and interest.
3) The **reward** (of lending money to the business) for the **investor** (shareholder) is a share **dividend**, often paid out twice a year. The investor can sell their shares at a **profit** if the share price goes up.
4) The **risk** to the **investor** is that the business may **fail**. When a business goes into **liquidation**, the shareholders lose most or all of their money.

High Gearing can be **Attractive** — during a **Growth** Phase

1) A firm that's trying to become the market leader, and has growing profits along with a strong product portfolio, may decide to borrow heavily in order to **fund expansion** and gain a **competitive advantage**.
2) When interest rates are very **low**, high gearing is less risky because interest payments are lower.
3) During times of **growth**, there are more profits left after paying loan interest and repayments.

There are **Various Methods** of **Reducing Gearing**

1) Gearing can be reduced by changes to the shareholders' funds. The firm could decide to issue more shares or retain more of its profits, for example.
2) Similarly, the firm could use alternative sources of finance to reduce its loans. It may decide to borrow via a **mortgage** that offers **lower interest payments** than an overdraft or loan. It could also renegotiate its existing loans (borrow over a longer or shorter period or from a different bank).
3) Other sources of finance could also be utilised such as **leasing**, accruals and current liabilities.

Financial Ratios: Profitability

Profitability ratios show profit margin. They compare profit with turnover and with capital employed.

Gross Profit Margin = Gross Profit ÷ Turnover × 100

1) The **gross profit margin** measures the relationship between the profits made and the amount of sales. It's expressed as a percentage, calculated by:

$$\text{Gross Profit Margin} = \frac{\text{Gross Profit}}{\text{Turnover}} \times 100$$

Gross profit = revenue – cost of sales.

Turnover = value of sales.

2) What counts as a good gross profit margin depends on the **type of business**. A business with a high asset turnover (e.g. a bakery) can afford to have low gross profit margin, but a higher figure is always preferable.
3) The ratio can be **improved** by either **increasing prices** or **reducing** the direct **cost of sales**.
4) A business can improve its overall gross profit margin by **stopping** selling products with a **low gross profit margin**.

Net Profit Margin = Net Profit ÷ Turnover × 100

Net profit = gross profit – indirect costs.

1) **Net profit ratio** doesn't include **overheads** (indirect costs). The ratio is again expressed as a percentage:

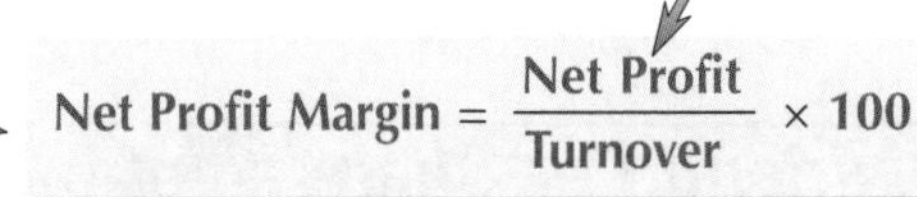

2) It's best to have a **high** net profit margin, although it does depend on the type of business, like the gross profit margin.
3) It's useful to **compare** net profit margin with gross profit margin over a **period of time**. The relationship between gross and net profit margins doesn't always work like you might expect — a price cut could reduce gross profit margin but increase the net profit margin. However, a business with a **declining net profit margin** compared to gross profit margin is having trouble with its **overheads**.
4) Net profit margin can be improved by **raising prices** or **lowering** cost of sales or (most importantly) **overheads**.

Return on Capital Employed (ROCE) is the most Important profitability ratio

1) The **return on capital employed** (ROCE) is considered to be the best way of analysing profitability. It's sometimes called the **primary efficiency ratio** and it's expressed as a percentage, calculated by:

The operating profit is found on the profit and loss account, see p.16.

$$\text{Return on Capital Employed} = \frac{\text{Operating Profit}}{\text{Capital Employed}} \times 100$$

Total capital employed = ordinary shares + preference shares + debentures + long term loans + reserves. It's found on the balance sheet.

2) The **ROCE** tells you how much money is **made** by the business, compared to how much money's been **put into** the business. It tells you how good the business is at generating profits from money invested.

There are several ways of calculating this ratio, but this method will get you through the exam.

3) A good **ROCE** is about **20%**, but 10-15% is OK. It's important to compare the ROCE with the Bank of England interest rate at the time because if the return is less than the interest rate they would have been better putting their money in the bank.
4) ROCE can be **improved** by **paying off debt** to reduce capital employed, or by making the business more **efficient** to **increase operating profit**.

Practice Questions

Q1 What's meant by "high gearing"?

Q2 Give two ways in which Return on Capital Employed can be improved.

Exam Questions

Q1 Evaluate the risks of investing in a business which has a high gearing ratio. (6 marks)

Q2 A business has sales revenue of £2 million. Its gross profit is £750 000, and its overheads are £250 000.
(a) Calculate the net profit ratio. (6 marks)
Answer on p.98.
(b) How might the business improve its net profit ratio? (6 marks)

Low gearing is also helpful when driving on icy roads...

Oh joy of joys, it's more ratios. You can probably guess what I'm going to say — learn the ratios carefully, don't get them mixed up, and be prepared to use them in the exam. You can get asked to carry out a specific ratio analysis, or you can get marks for choosing a good ratio yourself. But make sure you know how to interpret the answers from the ratios too.

Shareholders' Ratios

Shareholders use ratios to see how much dividend they'll get, and to see how the business is performing.

Investors *use* ***Ratio Analysis*** *to decide where to invest*

1) **Investors** use several financial ratios when making decisions about where to invest their money. These ratios are called **shareholders' ratios**.
2) **Dividends** are paid out to shareholders once or twice a year, out of the company's profits. **Ratios** help an investor to see the **rate of return** to expect — what proportion of its earnings a company uses to pay out in dividends.
3) Investors would also expect to see the price of their shares **increase** over time. A return on investment caused by a rise in the share price is called a **capital gain**.
4) Some investors want **short-term profits** which give them a quick return through **dividends**. Shareholders' ratios are most useful for these investors.
5) Other investors want a **long-term return** through **capital gain**. They'd want the company to invest profits in growth instead of paying them out as dividends.

What it's all about...

Dividend Per Share *= Total Dividend ÷ Number of Shares*

1) **Dividend per share** is usually stated at the foot of the **profit and loss** account (see p.17).
2) The amount of profit set aside for dividend payment is simply divided by the number of shares issued:
3) The resulting figure is usually expressed as a number of **pence**. Say the dividend per share is 9.5p and you own 1000 shares — you'd get a dividend cheque for £95.
4) Shareholders looking for **short-term return** want the dividend per share to be as **high** as possible. Shareholders looking for **long-term return** through capital gain might be happy with a **low** dividend per share.
5) It's pretty much OK for a company with a **low share price** to have a **low dividend per share** — this is because shareholders can afford to **buy more shares** to get the dividend return they want.
6) It's totally up to the **directors** how much profit they set aside for dividend payments, by the way. If the shareholders don't like it, they can vote at the AGM to sack the directors and bring in a new lot.

$$\text{Dividend Per Share} = \frac{\textbf{Total Dividend}}{\textbf{Number of Shares Issued}}$$

Dividend Yield *= Dividend Per Share ÷ Price Per Share × 100*

1) **Dividend yield** is a comparison between the cost of the shares and the dividend received. It's expressed as a percentage and calculated by:
2) Shareholders looking for **short-term return** want a **high dividend yield**.
3) Dividend yield and dividend share can both be improved by increasing the proportion of profits that are paid out as dividend.
4) Dividend yield depends on share price — which can go up and down, depending on business performance.

$$\text{Dividend Yield} = \frac{\textbf{Dividend Per Share}}{\textbf{Price Per Share}} \times 100$$

Example: Johan buys **100 shares** at **500p** each, and the dividend per share is **15p**.

$$\textbf{Dividend Yield} = \frac{15}{500} \times 100 = \mathbf{3\%}$$

3% really **isn't very good** for a short-term return. If he wants short-term profit, Johan ought to be looking at **other forms of investment** to see if he could earn more profit elsewhere — e.g. a savings account at the local bank.

Limitations of Ratios

***Ratio Analysis** has its **Limitations** — just like the final accounts do*

All financial **ratios** compare two figures from the **accounts**, and give you a raw **number** as an answer.

Ratios don't take account of any **non-numerical factors**, so although they can give you an idea of how a business is performing, they are not an absolute means of assessing a company's financial health. They have several limitations that you must able to evaluate in your exam answers:

1) **Internal strengths**, such as the quality of staff, don't appear on the accounts, so they won't come up in ratios.
2) **External factors**, such as the **economic** or **market** environment, aren't reflected in the accounts. When the market's very **competitive**, or the economy's in a **downturn**, it's OK for ratios to suffer a bit.
3) **Future changes** such as technological advances or changes in interest rates can't be predicted by the accounts, so they won't show up in the ratios.
4) Ratios only contain information about the **past** and **present**. A business which has **just started** investing for growth will have lousy ratios until the investment **pays off** — that doesn't mean it's not worth investing in.

Example of how ratio analysis can't predict changes in external factors

- Person A is interested in **investing** in XYZ Ltd. **Ratio analysis** indicates that XYZ is **performing strongly** and gives a **good rate of return** for the investor, so she decides to **buy 1000 shares.**
- Later that day, person A talks to person B, who says **new EU health and safety legislation** will **ban XYZ** from making any more of its products from next year onwards. XYZ Ltd must now either **diversify** into another product/service or **close.**
- Person A doesn't feel so clever about her investment now. XYZ Ltd will need **time** and **money** to **reinvest** in a new production line so **profits will be very scarce** for the next few months. Worse still, XYZ Ltd may decide to **close** and she'd have shares with **no value at all**. What a nightmare.

*When **Comparing** ratios, compare **Like** with **Like***

1) It's important to **compare** today's ratios with ratios for the same business over a period of time, to spot trends. These comparisons over time need to take account of **variable factors** — things which change over time, such as **inflation**, accounting procedures, the business activities of the firm and the market environment. These things won't always stay the same over the period that you're looking at.
2) It's also useful to compare ratios with **other businesses**, either in the same industry or in different industries. It's important to **compare like with like**. Other firms may **differ** in size, objectives and product portfolio. They may do their **accounts** differently, e.g. they may have their financial year end in a different month.

Practice Questions

Q1 Why might a shareholder not automatically want as high a dividend per share as possible?

Q2 Dividend yield is a better measure of performance than dividend share. Why is this?

Q3 Give a brief outline of two non-numerical factors that should be taken into account when doing ratio analysis.

Q4 Why might comparisons of today's ratios with last year's ratios be inaccurate?

Exam Questions

Q1 Net Profit: £500 000   Profit after tax: £300 000
Dividend per share: 6p   Shares issued: 100 000
If the share price is 300p, calculate the dividend yield. Answer on p.98. (6 marks)

Q2 Outline two external factors that should be taken into account when analysing financial ratios. (6 marks)

Q3 Ratio analysis gives information about the past.
Discuss what value ratio analysis has in predicting future performance. (12 marks)

My analysis is that this is all rather dull...

It's not possible to make 100% solid conclusions from ratio analysis alone. You need to use other data from several sources alongside ratios. SWOT and PEST (p.90) analysis are a good starting point — they consider the market that the business is trading in. Also, bear in mind that using data from the past isn't always a great way to predict the future. Stuff changes.

Contribution and Break-Even Analysis

Some of this is revision of AS content, and some is brand new content, so learn the lot.

Break-Even is the point where **Profit = 0** and **Loss = 0**

Definition: **Break-even** is the point where **total revenue = total costs**, so the business is making **no profit** and **no loss**. It's easy to see break even on a **graph**. Break-even graphs plot **revenue** and **total costs** against **output**. The point where revenue = total costs is the break-even point.

Example: A company has **variable costs** of **£10 per unit**, and sells each unit for **£30**. The fixed costs are **£600 000**.

1) The graph shows the **variable costs** of £10 per unit as a **red line**, and the **fixed costs** of £600 000 as a horizontal **blue line**.
2) The fixed and variable costs have been added together to give **total costs**, shown as a **purple line**.
3) The revenue of £30 per unit is shown as a **green line**.
4) The point where the revenue line and the total costs line meet is the **break-even point**. It's that simple.
5) The **margin of safety** is the difference between **current output** (sales) and **break-even output**. When the firm produces 35 000 units, the margin of safety is 5000 units.

Fixed costs are overheads, which don't vary when production is increased or decreased. Variable costs vary with the number of units produced.

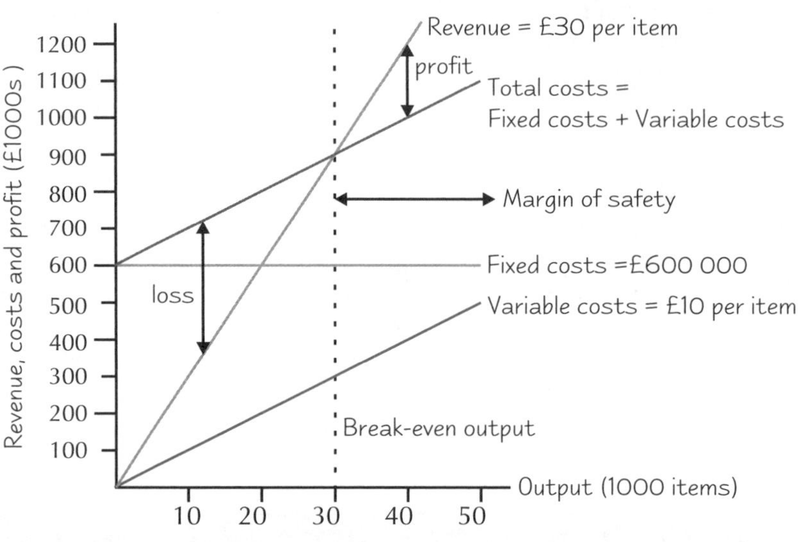

Break Even analysis shows what happens when **Costs** and **Prices Change**

1) The reason break-even analysis is so useful for businesses is because it allows them to **predict** the **change** in **profit levels** if there was a change in revenue or costs.
2) It can help managers to make **decisions** about **prices**, e.g. if managers want to increase or lower the price of a product, break even analysis shows them the effect this will have on total revenue and profit levels.
3) Break-even analysis can also help in **investment decision-making**. It shows the **impact** the investment would have on costs, revenue and profit.

Example 1: A company has **variable costs** of **£10 per unit**, and sells each unit for **£30**. The fixed costs were **£600 000**, but they're going to rise to **£700 000** because ground rents are increasing. Break-even rises to **35 000**.

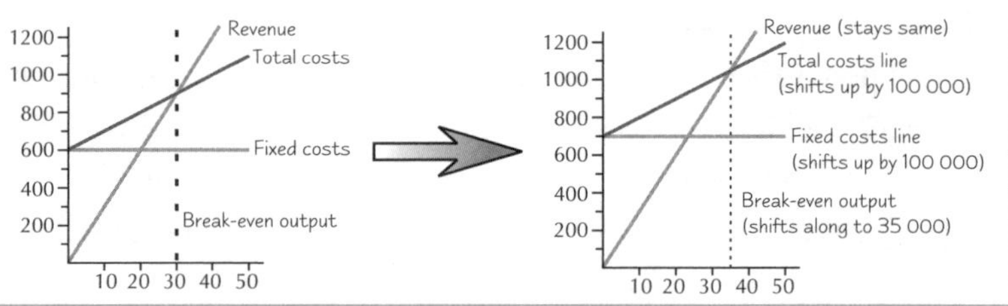

You can also **Calculate Break-Even** by working out **Contribution Per Unit**

1) The **contribution** that a unit makes toward the **profit** of a firm is the difference between the selling price of a product and the variable costs of making it.

   Contribution per unit = selling price per unit – variable costs per unit

2) Contribution is used to pay fixed costs. What's left over is profit.
3) **Break-even** is where **contribution from all sales** = **fixed costs**. Break-even output is fixed costs over contribution per unit:

$$\textbf{Break-even output} = \frac{\textbf{Fixed costs}}{\textbf{Contribution per unit}}$$

Example: A company has **variable costs** of **£10 per unit**, and sells each unit for **£30**. The fixed costs are **£600 000**.
Contribution = £20. (£30 – £10)
Break-even = 600 000 ÷ 20 = 30 000 sales

The contribution method is less fuss than the graph method, although neither method's exactly hard.

Contribution and Break-Even Analysis

Break-Even Analysis has *Limitations*

1) It assumes that the firm **sells everything** that it produces **without wastage**, which often isn't true.
2) It also assumes that **variable costs** vary in proportion to the level of output. Businesses can get **discounts** for **bulk purchases**, so their costs don't go up in direct proportion with output.
3) Break-even analysis is for **one product**. Most businesses sell **several products**, and a separate graph for each product would be needed to give an overall picture of the profitable output level. This would get **complicated**.

Contribution lets firms decide if it's *Worthwhile* to *Accept Special Orders*

Example: McCormack Textiles produces embroidered handbags and sells them for **£35 each**. The variable costs of producing each handbag are **£20**. A **national retailer** asks for **8000 units** at **£25 each**. The burning question is, should McCormack Textiles Ltd accept the order?

1) Even though the firm wouldn't make as much **profit** per item as usual, they'd still earn a **contribution** from each item. Each handbag would earn a **contribution** of **£5** (£25 price – £20 variable costs). The whole order would earn a contribution of **£40 000** (£5 × 8000).
2) McCormack Textiles Ltd would **probably** accept the order, so long as the **fixed costs** of producing the handbags don't go up. Say the firm has to rent **extra factory space** the fixed costs would go up — so long as the fixed costs go up by **less than the contribution**, it's worth taking the order.
3) **Variable costs** might go up as well. McCormack Textiles Ltd might have to pay its workers overtime, which would increase the variable costs. This would mean that the special order would make **less contribution**.
4) McCormack Textiles Ltd might decide to go ahead with the order even if it doesn't make a contribution, if they reckon that exposure to a wider market will result in **higher demand** for their handbags and more sales.

Even special one-off orders at **higher** prices than usual might not be worth accepting. An order that needs to be filled very quickly would need **extra workers**, **overtime payments** and maybe **extra factory space**. It's possible that **costs** might rise by enough to make the order not worth taking.

Contribution can help a business decide what to *Make*

1) The decision to **delete** a product from a company's portfolio is partly based on its **contribution** to profit and the level of **output** required to **break even**. A **high break-even output** uses lots of **resources**, which could be put to better use **elsewhere** in the company. It's better to use resources where they earn contribution.
2) Other factors such as **customer goodwill** and **employee morale** should be taken into account before deciding to delete a product. Deleting a product might turn **previously loyal** customers off the whole product portfolio.
3) A **manufacturer** which assembles components into a finished item may decide to **produce** some components itself and to **buy** others in from **outside**. The decision of which to buy and which to make is based on contribution. For each component, given the fixed and variable costs of making it and the fixed costs of buying it, you can work out break-even — the amount where the costs of buying and making would be the same.

Practice Questions

Q1 Write down the equation for calculating break even from contribution.

Q2 What happens to break even output when (a) fixed costs rise? (b) variable costs rise? (c) the selling price rises?

Q3 Give one benefit and one limitation of break-even analysis.

Q4 Outline the circumstances where a firm should accept a one-off order at less than the usual selling price.

Exam Question

Q1 Clough's make sieves at a variable cost of £3 per unit. Their fixed costs are £20 000 per year. They sell at £5 per unit. The Clough's factory is currently operating at 90% capacity.
(a) How many sieves would they have to sell to break even? (6 marks)
(b) Clough's get an order from a big retailer for 4000 sieves at £3.75 each. Should they take the order? (8 marks)

Answer on p.98.

Well, here's my two pennies' worth...

Contribution is a very useful little thing. It comes up in pricing, it's used to work out break even, it's used to help decide whether to accept one-off orders, or whether to stop making a product. So, you ought to be able to work out contribution. Beware though, contribution calculations don't give you the final answer for special orders — there are other factors.

Cash Flow Forecasts

Cash Flow is the movement of cash in and out of a business. Cash flow forecasts predict when businesses might have money problems.

There's a **Delay** between **Paying** for **Supplies** and **Getting Paid** for **Goods**

1) A firm supplying its customers with goods on credit will have to **wait** to be paid for those goods.
2) While it's waiting the firm still has to pay for **overheads** and **raw materials**, so it's paying out money every month while it waits to receive money from its debtors.
3) If the business runs out of money to pay its creditors before its debtors pay up, and can't pay its creditors, it will become **insolvent** (limited liability company) or **bankrupt** (sole trader or partnership).
4) Being able to **forecast** cash flow is vital to business survival and the decision-making process.

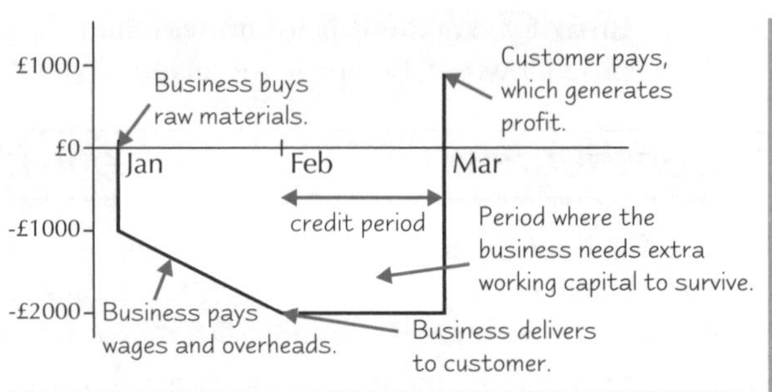

Cash Flow Forecasts Predict when cash will **Come In** and **Go Out**

1) **Cash flow forecasts** are usually done on a **monthly** basis.
2) Managers can **predict** when they'll be short of cash, and **arrange loans** or **overdrafts** in time to avoid problems.
3) They can also predict when they'll be rolling in cash. Spare cash could be better used to invest in fixed assets or pay creditors.
4) Businesses show a cash flow forecast to **financial institutions** when trying to get a loan, overdraft, or mortgage. The cash flow forecast serves as **proof of ability to pay** in the future and proof that the firm is **well managed**.
5) **Venture capitalists** like to see a cash flow forecast before investing in a business.
6) **Suppliers** offering **credit** or **hire purchase** may also expect to see a cash flow statement.
7) Businesses have to predict their cash flow based on sales predictions and predictions of costs. It's generally easier to predict costs than it is to predict sales.

Example: Here's a **sample cash flow forecast** for a business. The business predicts its April and May revenue to be £20 000, rising to £30 000 in June and £35 000 in July. Costs are expected to be £17 000 in April and June, £22 000 in May and £20 000 in June. The business starts April with £5 000 in the bank.

Things are looking pretty good come July — but remember, it's **only a forecast**...

	Item	**Apr**	**May**	**Jun**	**Jul**
Cash in	**Total revenue**	**£20 000**	**£20 000**	**£30 000**	**£35 000**
Cash out	Wages and rent	£15 000	£15 000	£15 000	£15 000
	Other costs	£2 000	£7 000	£2 000	£5 000
	Total costs	**£17 000**	**£22 000**	**£17 000**	**£20 000**
Net monthly cash flow	**Net cash flow**	**£3 000**	**(£2 000)**	**£13 000**	**£15 000**
	Opening balance	£5 000	£8 000	£6 000	£19 000
	Closing balance	**£8 000**	**£6 000**	**£19 000**	**£34 000**

Getting **Cash Flow Forecasts Wrong** has **Consequences**

1) Cash flow forecasts predict when the business will need a **loan** to keep it afloat. Getting this wrong on the over-optimistic side can result in the business running out of working capital, and becoming **insolvent** or **bankrupt**.
2) **Potential lenders** like to see a nice **healthy cash flow forecast**, because they want to be confident that the business will have **enough cash coming in** to pay off a loan. A cash flow forecast that's **too pessimistic** will result in the business securing **less investment** or loan capital than it could have done.

Cash Flow Forecasts

Cash Flow Forecasts can't be 100% Accurate

1) The **reliability** of any forecast **depends hugely** on the **quality** of the **data** used in its construction. Garbage in, garbage out.
2) Data relating to **overheads** such as electricity bills must be accurate. It's much **easier** for an **established business** to get these right than it is for a **new start-up**. An established business can **assume** that this year's electricity bill is going to be pretty much the same as last year's (bar expansion, or electricity price rises). A new start-up has to **estimate** their electricity usage from **scratch**.
3) Cash flow forecasts are based on **assumptions** about **future sales** and **future costs**, and these need to be **realistic**. Managers are often **over optimistic** about future trading.
4) The **market changes** all the time. The more uncertain the market, and the **faster** it changes, the **harder** it is to **forecast** sales and costs accurately to produce a decent cash flow forecast.

Gerald was always prepared for inaccurate forecasts.

Internal factors can change after the forecast's been made.

1) **Machinery** can break down. This **damages productivity** and **revenue**. It also requires expensive repairs, which will **increase costs**.
2) Skilled **staff** may leave the company, again damaging **productivity** and **revenue**.

External situations can also change after the forecast's been made.

1) **Suppliers** may **increase prices**. This affects **direct costs**, so **cash outflows** will definitely be altered. The business may change its **selling prices** to compensate, which can have a knock-on effect on **sales revenue**, so **cash inflows** may be altered as well. **Profits** will be altered by this.
2) **Competitors** may **decrease prices**, which affects **demand**. **Pricing policy** may also be affected, which has knock-on effects on **cash inflow**, **sales revenue** and **profit**.
3) **Technology** may advance more rapidly than planned. This may affect **market demand** and sales revenue, and may require money to be spent on new product development.
4) The **economy** can change. **Interest rates** can **go up**, which would **increase costs** related to loan repayments and interest on overdrafts.

The **closer** a firm's **cash flow statement** at the end of the year is to what their **cash flow forecast** was at the beginning of the year, the **better** that firm **understands what they're doing**, and the better they **understand the market they're in**.

Practice Questions

Q1 Why would a firm produce a cash flow forecast when applying for credit?

Q2 How would you work out the closing balance in a cash flow forecast?

Q3 Give an example of an internal factor which could alter the cash flow forecast.

Q4 How could a change in the economy effect a company's cash flow forecast?

Exam Questions

Q1 "It's not worth producing a cash flow forecast if it's going to be inaccurate." Discuss. (10 marks)

Q2 Explain two ways in which changes in the market and the economy can affect the accuracy of a cash flow forecast. (8 marks)

I wonder how "psychic medium" businesses do at cash flow forecasts...

Customers push for longer credit periods, suppliers push to get paid sooner, and bank managers don't like businesses to run up a massive overdraft. It's best to see the rock and the hard place coming before you get squished in between them. Unfortunately, the accuracy of cash flow predictions depends on the market, which is notoriously unpredictable.

Investment Appraisals

Investment appraisal helps businesses decide what projects to invest in, in order to get the best, fastest, least risky return for their money.

Investment** decisions must balance **Risk** and **Return

1) **Investment** can mean buying shares in a business (external investment). It can also be internal investment — buying a large **asset**, spending money on **promotion**, **expanding** into an overseas market, reorganising, or developing a **new brand**. Any situation where you need to **spend money** in order to **make money** is investment.
2) Any situation where you have to spend money in order to make money has **risk**. Both external and internal investors like the risks to be low and the return (profit) to be high.
3) There are a number of **investment appraisal tools** used to gauge the **risk** and **reward** of the available projects. All of these methods are useful, but they're only as good as the **data** used to calculate them.
4) Investment appraisal methods assess how much **profit** a project is going to make, and how **fast** the money will come in. The faster money comes in, the less risk in the long run.

Payback** measures the **Length of Time** it takes to **Get Your Money Back

1) **Payback period** is the time it takes for the project to make enough money to pay back the initial investment, calculated by:

$$\frac{\text{Cost of investment}}{\text{Contribution of investment to profit per year}}$$

2) For example, a £2 million project that has an annual profit prediction of £250,000 will reach payback in 8 years (£2 million ÷ £0.25 million = 8).
3) Managers compare this payback period with other projects and choose which project to go ahead with.

Advantages of Payback Period Calculation:	It's easy to calculate and understand. It's very good for high risk or high tech projects.
Disadvantages of Payback Period Calculation:	It ignores cash flow after payback. It ignores the time value of money.

Wondering what the blue cheese that's about? See next page...

Average Rate of Return** (ARR) compares **Yearly Profit** with **Investment

1) **Average rate of return** (ARR) compares the **average annual profit** with the level of investment.
2) The higher the ARR, the more **favourable** the project will appear.
3) ARR is expressed as a **percentage** and calculated by:

$$\frac{\text{Average Annual Profit}}{\text{Investment}} \times 100 = X\%$$

Example:

	Investment	Year 1	Year 2	Year 3	Year 4	Year 5
Project A	(£10M)	£4M	£5M	£6M	£7M	£5M
Project B	(£8M)	£3M	£3M	£4M	£6M	£6M

These are the expected profits for each year.

The payback period for both these projects is the same, so you need to use Average rate of return.

Project A pays back during year 3. It costs £10M, by the end of year 2 it's returned £9M and by the end of year 3 it's returned £15M. Project B also pays back its £8M investment some time in year 3.

Project A (£10M investment) has a profit of (£M) 4 + 5 + 6 + 7 + 5 = £27M.

Average annual profit is £27M divided by the five years = £5.4M

ARR = £5.4M / £10M investment x 100% = 54%

Project B (£8M investment) has a profit of (£M) 3 + 3 + 4 + 6 + 6 = £22M

Average annual profit is £22M ÷ 5 years = £4.4M

ARR = £4.4M / £8M investment x 100% = 55%

The managers would choose project B because it has a higher ARR, just. Just. By a whisker.

Advantages of Average Rate of Return:	It's easy to calculate and understand. It takes account of all the project's cash flows.
Disadvantages of Average Rate of Return:	It ignores the timing of the cash flows. It ignores the time value of money.

Investment Appraisals

The *Future Value* of cash inflow depends on *Risk* and *Opportunity Cost*

If someone offers you £100 cash in hand **now** or in one year's time, you'd do best to take it now. This is called the **time value of money**. It's the principle of money being worth less if you wait for it, because of risk and opportunity cost.

1) There's a **risk** that the person would never pay you the £100 after a year had gone by.
2) In a year's time it'd be worth less due to **inflation**. You wouldn't be able to buy as much stuff with that £100.
3) There's an **opportunity cost** — you could **invest** the money instead of **waiting** for it. A high interest account would beat the rate of inflation and give you **even more value** than the £100 in your hand today.
4) You could invest **£100** in an account giving you **6% APR interest**, and you'd get **£106** at the end of the year. If you invested **£94.34** in an account giving you 6% interest you'd get **£100** at the end of the year. So, if you assume an investment interest rate of **6%**, the value of **£100** paid to you at the **end of the year** is the same as **£94.34 today**.

A payment after a year or two, or three, is **always worth less** than the **same payment** made to you **today**.

Discounting adjusts the value of *Future Cash Inflows* to their *Present Value*

1) **Discounting** is the process of **adjusting the value of money** received in the **future** to its **present value**. It's done so that investors can **compare like with like** when they look at the cash inflows they'll receive from projects. £4 million this year **isn't the same** as £4 million in five years' time, and it's not wise to **pretend** that it is the same.
2) **Discounting** can be seen as the **opposite** of **calculating interest**.
3) It's done by **multiplying** the amount of money by a **discount factor**. This discount factor is like the opposite of a bank interest rate. Discount factors are **always less than 1**, because the value of money in the future is always less than its value now.

4) **Discount factors** depend on what the **interest rate** is predicted to be. **High** interest rates mean that the future payments have to be **discounted a lot** to give the correct present values. This is so that the present value represents the **opportunity cost** of not investing the money in the **bank** where it'd earn a nice **high interest rate**.
5) As you might expect, when **interest rates** are predicted to be **low**, the future cash inflow needn't be discounted so much. There's less opportunity cost.
6) Discounting is also related to the **risk** element of a project. There's a **risk** that the **project won't pay out** the expected returns, because of market changes.

Year	0	1	2	3	4	5
Discount Value for 10% interest	1	0.909	0.826	0.751	0.683	0.621
Present Value of £1000	£1000	£909	£826	£751	£683	£621

Year 1 discount value = 100/110 = 0.909. Year 2 discount value = $(100/110)^2$ = 0.826. Year 3 discount value = $(100/110)^3$ = 0.751. It's like compound interest in reverse.

Practice Questions

Q1 What does ARR take account of that payback doesn't?

Q2 Give one advantage and one disadvantage of ARR.

Q3 How does risk help to explain why the value of £1000 paid in two years' time isn't the same as £1000 paid today?

Q4 What is discounting, and what's it kind of the opposite of?

Exam Questions

Answer on p.98.

Q1 A business is investing in a new product. The initial investment is £200 000. The product will generate revenue of £100 000 per year, and costs of £60 000 per year. Calculate the average rate of return on the investment. (6 marks)

Q2 Explain why a future cash inflow must be discounted to give its present value. (6 marks)

You have to speculate if you want to accumulate...

The idea that money is worth less if you have to wait for it almost certainly seems, oh I don't know, really freaking strange. There really is good value to this "time value of money" — there's the risk involved in waiting to be paid, and there's the opportunity cost of what you could have done with the money if you had it in your hand from the start.

Investment Appraisals

One last page of investment appraisal calculations, and then a page about why investment appraisal calculations aren't "all that and a bag o' chips" after all.

Discounted Cash Flow allows for Risk, Inflation and Opportunity Cost

1) **Discounted cash flow** (DCF) is an investment appraisal tool that allows for money to change value over **time**.
2) It's used to calculate the **Net Present Value** (NPV) of the cash flowing into a project. This is the amount of money it'd be worth if you had it **now**, which is **always** less than its face value.
3) The **Net Present Value** is worked out by multiplying the cash inflow by a **discount factor**. (See p.35.)
4) The **discount factor** applied is the **required rate of return** for the projects — the rate of return that the managers decide that they need to get from the project to make it worthwhile. The **discount factor** will be **supplied for you** in the exam, so you won't need to work this out — thank all that's good and chocolatey.
5) The **downsides** of DCF are that it's a bit **hard to calculate**, and that it's hard to figure out what the **discount factor** ought to be. The longer the project is set to last, the harder it is to predict the discount factor.

Example:
Apply the discount factor of **10%** to the same figures as the example on p.34.

Project A	Cash inflow	Discount Value (10%)	Present Value
Year 1	£4M	0.909	£4M × 0.909 = £3 636 000
Year 2	£5M	0.826	£5M × 0.826 = £4 130 000
Year 3	£6M	0.751	£6M × 0.751 = £4 506 000
Year 4	£7M	0.683	£7M × 0.683 = £4 781 000
Year 5	£5M	0.621	£5M × 0.621 = £3 105 000
Total Present Value of Cash Inflows			£20 158 000
Net Present Value (total minus Investment)			-£10M = **£10 158 000**
Project B	**Cash inflow**	**Discount Value (10%)**	**Present Value**
Year 1	£3M	0.909	£3M × 0.909 = £2 727 000
Year 2	£3M	0.826	£3M × 0.826 = £2 478 000
Year 3	£4M	0.751	£4M × 0.751 = £3 004 000
Year 4	£6M	0.683	£6M × 0.683 = £4 098 000
Year 5	£6M	0.621	£6M × 0.621 = £3 726 000
Total Present Value of Cash Inflows			£16 033 000
Net Present Value (total minus Investment)			-£8M = **£8 033 000**

Year 1 discount value = 100/110 = 0.909

Year 2 discount value = $(100/110)^2$ = 0.826

Year 3 discount value = $(100/110)^3$ = 0.751

Remember, project A had an initial investment of £10M.

Project B had an initial investment of £8M.

Using this method of investment appraisal the business would choose Project A because the profits are bigger in the early years and this is when the NPV is bigger.

Internal Rate of Return (IRR) works out Several NPVs

1) **Internal Rate of Return** (IRR) is concerned with the **break even rate of return** of the project.
2) It uses **DCF** to produce **several net present values** for each project, each at **slightly different discount rates**, until they get an **NPV** of **zero.** The discount rate which gives a NPV of zero is called the **internal rate of return**.
3) Managers know that the **internal rate of return** needs to be higher than the **expected rate of interest**, otherwise they might as well put the money in the **bank** instead of investing it in the project.
4) Managers can also set their own "**criterion level discount rate**" which is their **minimum rate of return**. Projects which have an **internal rate of return** lower than this criterion level don't get the go-ahead.
5) Calculating the IRR is **really hard**, and there's a lot of repetition involved. It's best done by **computer**.

Advantages of Internal Rate of Return:	It allows you to set the **required rate of return**. It allows for the **time value of money**.
Disadvantages of Internal Rate of Return:	The calculation requires **computers**. Some managers find it **hard** to get their heads around it.

Investment Appraisals

Non-Numerical, Qualitative** factors affect **Investment Decisions

The investment decisions made by managers are based upon a wide range of numerical data and quantitative methods. Managers must also put the decisions into a **qualitative** context, based on internal factors and market uncertainty.

Business Objectives and Strategy Can Influence Investment Decisions

1) An investment appraisal recommended purely on financial data **may not fit in** with the **objectives** of a firm. Many businesses will only make an investment if the project will **help them achieve** their objectives.
2) For example, a business which aims to produce **low cost products** for a large mass market (e.g. teaspoons) would be unlikely to invest **as much** in **research and development** as a high-end technology business.
3) **Human resources investment** takes away from short term profit, so a firm with the objective of **maximising profit** for shareholder dividends would be unlikely to invest in staff development. On the other hand, a business which aims to produce **high quality**, high tech products would invest in **skilled staff**.

Corporate Image Can Influence Investment Decisions

1) **Good corporate image** brings **customer goodwill** and **loyalty** in the long term, and the firm may consider this more important than **short term rate of return** on investment. Investment decisions that create bad publicity and damage customer loyalty will damage the bottom line in the **long term**.
2) A firm with a green, **ecologically friendly** image would avoid investments that would damage the environment. Some firms incorporate environmental costs into their investment appraisals.

Human Relations can Influence Investment Decisions

1) Investments which result in a **loss of jobs** may be turned down, even if they show a good rate of return.
2) **Loss of jobs** affects **staff morale**. Cost of **redundancy payments** should be factored into the decision. Trade unions may **strike** over the job losses, which would affect **productivity**. **Corporate image** may also be damaged.

Risk is Always at Work in the Market — and Each Project Has a Risk of Failure

1) The market is an environment that has **risk** and **uncertainty** every day. **Exchange rates** may alter, **sales** may decrease/increase, **customers' tastes** may change and **competitors** may become stronger.
2) Also, **each project** has specific **risk** — a new product might not sell very well. Branching into a new market is risky and might not pay off. Every firm has a **different attitude** to **risk**.

*Wrapping it all up — these **Investment Decisions** are **Hard...***

Investors have to make decisions about which firm to buy shares in. They use **ratio analysis**, **market trend analysis**, awareness of **product life cycle** and the **industry lifecycle** to arrive at their decision.

Managers of firms must also make **investment decisions** about which **projects** would be best for the future of the firm, set against the business **objectives**, **corporate image** and attitude to **risk**.

At this level you'll need to draw on all your **accumulated knowledge** of business to give the examiner some proper **critical analysis** and well thought out **evaluation**. Good analysis and evaluation will get you the **higher level marks**.

Practice Questions

Q1 What are the main advantages and disadvantages of DCF?

Q2 What's IRR stand for, and what the heck is it, anyway?

Q3 Give examples of three qualitative factors that affect investment decisions.

Exam Question

Answer on p.98.

Q1 Denton Ceramics are considering investing in a new kiln. The kiln will cost £17 000, and will generate £5000 extra revenue a year for 5 years. Calculate the NPV of the project, given a discount factor of 5%. (8 marks)

Ow, my head hurts...

Quantitative methods using calculations to appraise investment decisions can be great because they give you answers that are easy to understand and compare. However, these calculations are only as good as the figures used in them — poor figures will give unrealistic answers. Also there are lots of other factors the calculations don't show, like the market situation.

Communication

Communication is vital in business, just to get the job done properly.
There's a link between motivation and communication, too.

There are several Categories of Communication

1) **Formal communications** are **officially endorsed** by the business. They include corporate notice boards, company newsletters, letters from managers or the HR department.
2) **Informal communications** are unofficial, e.g. gossip, emails between employees and leaked information.
3) **Vertical communication** travels **up** and **down** the hierarchy. **Authoritarian** corporate cultures often only have downward communication — but a mixture of upward and downward communication is best.
4) **Horizontal** (**lateral**) communication occurs between staff on the **same level** within the hierarchy.
5) **Internal communication** remains within the organisation, e.g. office notice board, internal email.
6) **External communication** is aimed at **external stakeholders**, e.g. websites, press releases.

Good Communication improves Business Efficiency

1) **Clear communication** reduces mistakes, saving time and money.
2) Clear, **effective communication** makes sure that all employees know what their **objectives** are.
3) **Fast**, **effective communication** can speed up decision-making, keep a business ahead of competitors, and reduce lead times for new products. This is **essential** in a fast-changing market such as IT or fashion.
4) Good communication **develops relationships** within the business, which helps encourage **commitment** to the business and increase employee motivation.

Modern business techniques require good communication

1) **Just In Time** production requires very **fast, effective communication** of **stock needs**.
2) **Kaizen** (continuous improvement) requires **two-way internal communication**. Employees and managers need to clearly and **effectively communicate** ways of improving.
3) **Delegation** requires **clear communication** — the task being delegated needs to be **clearly defined**, so that the employee knows exactly what they've got responsibility for.
4) **Quality circles** are groups of employees from **different departments** who meet to discuss **quality issues**. Communication within a quality circle **obviously** has to be effective.

Communication is important within Work Groups

1) Communication isn't just between head office and managers, or between managers and underlings. Employees who **work together** communicate as part of their work, and as part of their "group dynamic".
2) Verbal and non-verbal communication within a group reinforces **group norms**. Group norms are the **habits** of the group that members must **stick to** — for example "everyone takes their turn to make tea for the group".
3) The way that people **behave** within a **group** can have an effect on the **whole organisation**. A group that doesn't **get on well** together won't achieve as much as a group where people get on smoothly.
4) There are **informal groups** at work, e.g. groups of friends — as well as formal job-related groups. Employees like the **social interaction** they get from both formal and informal groups.

Motivation improves Communication

1) **Motivated** workers have the **confidence to** communicate with their **superiors**, and suggest ways of improving performance.
2) Modern work practices such as **kaizen** and employee empowerment require **constant communication**. **Motivated** workers are likely to **volunteer** to take part in **kaizen groups** and **quality circles.**
3) **Demotivated** people don't care enough to communicate, which can cause inefficiency and other problems like poor quality and bad customer service.
4) **Demotivated** workers tend to **ignore** communication, especially if they think it might **increase their workload**.

Communication

Communication improves Motivation — it goes both ways

1) **Communication** is needed to keep employees **motivated**. Employees need to be told what they're supposed to be doing, and they need to be told when they've done a good job.
2) People who don't communicate feel **isolated** and **demotivated**, this is usually bad for the business.
3) **Autocratic** managers only believe in one-way communication. Not being **listened** to is **demotivating.**
4) **Modern work practices** such as kaizen and delegation can **improve motivation**, but they **require good communication** to work properly.

1) **Elton Mayo** found that people achieved more when they got **positive attention**.
2) Mayo thought managers should **pay attention** to workers as individuals, and **involve** them in decision making. This required increased and improved **internal communication.**

1) **Maslow's hierarchy of needs** identifies **social needs**, **self-esteem** and **self-actualisation** as the three highest level needs. Communication is necessary to fulfil all three.
2) Workers need to communicate to meet their **social needs.**
3) **Two way communication** between managers and workers is necessary to give workers **responsibility** and **recognition**, which helps meet their **self esteem needs**.
4) Two way communication is vital to allow workers to fulfil their **potential** and meet their **self-actualisation needs.**

1) Poor relationships with peers and managers are often caused by **poor communication.** **Herzberg** suggests hygiene factors such as relationships need satisfying **before** motivation is possible.
2) **Personal development** and **recognition of achievement** are motivating factors, and they both require two-way communication between worker and manager.

Feedback tells the Sender that the Message has been Received

1) **Two-way communication** involves **feedback**. A **discussion** between a manager and subordinates about a new policy is two-way communication.
2) **One-way communication** doesn't have feedback. A notice on the **staff noticeboard** is one-way communication.

Two-way communication
sender ⟺ reciever

One-way communication
sender ⟹ receiver

1) Giving **feedback** after communication lets the sender know that the receiver has **got the message** and understood it. This helps the sender **assess** their communication.
2) Feedback allows the receiver to **ask questions** about the message, and ask for clarification if they didn't understand the message.
3) Feedback can also take the form of **discussion**.

Practice Questions

Q1 What is the difference between horizontal communication and vertical communication?

Q2 Give two examples of ways that motivation can improve communication.

Q3 Give two reasons why communication is necessary to fulfil the top level needs in Maslow's hierarchy of needs.

Q4 What is feedback? How does feedback help communication?

Exam Question

Q1 Use relevant theory to explain why effective communication between managers and their employees often leads to improved staff motivation. (8 marks)

Have a cup of tea and a chat — it's good for morale...

You'll have studied motivation for AS level, and now it's time to see how motivation is linked to good communication. It goes both ways — poor morale affects communication, and poor communication lowers morale. It's important you can put communication into context, and spot where it can be improved in any business case study that you get in the exam.

Communication

Good communication isn't always plain sailing. There are barriers to communication, which need to be sorted out.

*Organisations must **Overcome** four **Barriers** that **Threaten Communication***

1 Attitudes

1) The receiver may be distracted by other responsibilities, and feel too busy to pay attention.
2) The receiver may **dislike** the sender, or may feel **threatened** by the communication.
3) Some **management styles** (e.g. the Autocratic style) discourage two-way internal communication.
4) Managers may be **unaware** of communication problems caused by organisational structure or management style. They may **assume** that the business has no communication problems.

2 Intermediaries

1) The **longer** the **chain of communication**, the more **mangled** and **garbled** the message can get between sender and receiver.
2) It can take a **long time** for a message to get from one end of a chain of command to the other.

3 Language barriers

1) A word can mean different things in different **cultures** — this includes business cultures as well as different nationalities. **Factory floor staff** may use language in a different way from higher management.
2) **Translation** into different languages can **distort meaning**. This is a problem for international businesses.
3) **Technical jargon** can be **complicated** and **confusing**.

4 Lack of sense of purpose

1) People who **don't understand why** they're being told something may **ignore** the messages.
2) The more **unfocused** messages the reciever gets, the more likely they are to **discard all messages** from the sender. This is often a problem with **external communication** from business to customer.

Noise** is anything that **Interferes** with **Communication

1) **Examples** of noise include: ⟶
   - **actual noise**, e.g. from factory **machines**.
   - **technical jargon** used in specialist industries, e.g. pharmaceuticals.
   - too many people trying to **talk at once** and not listening to others.
   - **"junk"** communication such as **spam emails**.
2) Noise should be **minimised** wherever possible — this **reduces** the potential for messages to be **misunderstood**.

***ICT** can **Improve** or **Worsen Communication** at work*

1) **Information communication technology** (ICT) can improve communication through activities such as **email** and **intranet** sites (like a website but only accessible from computers physically linked to each other within the organisation). Benefits of these methods include the **speed** and **ease** with which messages can be sent.
2) **Databases** can be used to communicate key data to managers. They can produce instant reports which contain data such as sales revenue or productivity figures. These are called **management information systems** (MIS).
3) Care must be taken not to **swamp** managers with too much information. This is called **communication overload**. Email, in particular, proliferates like mad — emails get forwarded and copied and sent back and forth.
4) Unlike **phone** conversations, **email** doesn't have **tone of voice**. Emails can be misread as "snarky". Email isn't as **formal** as written memos and letters, so it's easier to **slip up** and write something unintentionally snotty.

<u>Case Study — Phones4U banned internal email</u>

⟵ Few businesses would go this far.

Problem: Phones4U found that store managers spent so much time reading emails that they were neglecting their staff and customers. Bosses estimated that 3 hours a day were being spent on email.

Solution: The company banned email for internal communication. Head office communicated to managers and staff via the corporate intranet. Employees were encouraged to use the phone or have face-to-face meetings.

Communication

Size has an **Impact** on **Communication**

Effective communication is **harder** in large companies as more messages need to reach more staff.

Communication overload is where there are too many messages

1) **Important** points get **lost** in a sea of messages.
2) **Reading lots of messages** takes **time** away from **other work duties**.
3) It's important to carefully weigh up the need for new communication systems before implementing them, as they may create communication overload.

Poor communication is a diseconomy of scale.

The more layers of hierarchy, the harder it is to communicate

1) **Rapid growth** often creates organisational structures with long **chains of command**. Long chains of command with many **intermediaries** make communication difficult.
2) It can take a long time for a message to get from one end of a chain of command to the other.
3) Messages can become **garbled** as they go along a chain of communication.

Large businesses may rely too much on written communication

1) It's not practical to have the same phone conversation with 50 people. It's much easier to send round a **memo**, or send an **email** to all 50 people.
2) One problem with this is that people sometimes **don't read memos** and group emails properly.
3) Also, if a recipient has a **question**, they'll have to send a note or email back. **Back and forth email conversations** take **longer** than **phone** conversations.
4) You don't even want to **think** about what happens when one of the recipients hits **"reply all"** to ask the sender a question. **Everyone** gets **another email** they don't want, and **wastes time** reading it or replying to it.

Multinational corporations have to overcome **cultural** and **language** barriers when communicating across **international borders** as well as practical constraints such as **time differences**.

Rapid growth can mean that a lot of new staff are recruited at once. **Inexperienced** new staff take time to get to grips with the communication system in a business. It isn't always immediately obvious **who to contact** about a problem.

Decentralisation can **Help** by making **Communication Chains Shorter**

1) **Decentralisation** (sharing out authority with junior employees) makes communication chains **shorter**, which makes them more **manageable**.
2) Lots of communication still goes on in a decentralised organisation. Good communication prevents inconsistencies developing between different departments and sectors of a decentralised business.
3) Managers and staff can also be **trained** in **communication skills** to help them cope.

Practice Questions

Q1 What are the four key barriers to communication? Give an example of each.

Q2 Give an example of one way that ICT can help communication, and one way that it can hinder communication.

Q3 How can decentralisation improve communication?

Exam Questions

Q1 The managing director of Argyll Biscuits doesn't like holding large meetings, and prefers to limit discussion and decision making to senior management. She believes line managers should pass on decisions made by senior management to lower level workers. Explain why Argyll Biscuits might have communication problems. (8 marks)

Q2 Explain whether there is a single best way for a banking firm to communicate with their customers. (6 marks)

Natter natter natter natter natter...

Managers and staff have to communicate with each other to get the job done properly. There's also communication between the business and its customers and suppliers to think about. Getting communication right isn't always easy. You'll have to be able to put these communication facts and ideas into context in a question you get in the exam.

Employer/Employee Relations

Good employer/employee relations are plain good business sense.

Employers and **Employees** need to **Cooperate** with each other

1) Employers and employees **need each other**.
2) **Employers** need **hard-working staff** to contribute to the production of a good or service that can be sold for a profit.
3) **Employees** need a **secure income** to support themselves and their families.
4) However, there's scope for **conflict** between them.
5) Employers would prefer to pay **lower wages** to keep **costs** down.
6) Employees want **higher wages** to improve their **standard of living**.

The two sides must **negotiate** to reach an **acceptable compromise** on wage rates, working conditions and terms of employment. **Failure** to reach agreement could lead to a **production stoppage**, and **both parties would suffer**.

A **successful** employer/employee relationship **maximises** the **cooperation** and **minimises** the potential for **conflict** between these two groups.

Collective Bargaining is done by **Large Groups** of employees

1) In most cases **individuals** don't negotiate their own rate of pay with their employer.
2) Negotiation is often done by a **trade union** or **professional association**, representing a group of employees and negotiating pay and working conditions **on their behalf**. The union **bargains collectively** for them all with their employer. Trade unions are sometimes called **"organised labour"**.
3) The result is a **common pay structure**, which is often called the **"going rate"** for the job. The employer wouldn't be able to pay anyone less than this going rate without the union kicking up a stink about it.
4) Employees and unions prefer **collective bargaining**, because it strengthens their position at the bargaining table and prevents **"divide and rule"** tactics by employers.

Collective bargaining does create some **problems**, though...

1) Having a single wage rate makes it **difficult** to **reward** variations in work **effort** between staff doing jobs with a similar rate of pay. This may **reduce** the levels of **motivation** if good staff are not recognised and rewarded.
2) In some large companies, the collectively bargained rate of pay covers employees working in **different factories and offices** scattered in **different locations** across the country. This one-wage-for-all approach doesn't recognise differences between different parts of the country — e.g. cost of living, house prices, level of unemployment, or even the local wages paid by other employers. A **variation** in wage rates to take account of these factors might be more appropriate.

Bargaining can also be done by **Small Groups** or **Individual Employees**

1) In recent years there's been a shift **away** from **collective bargaining** towards **individual** and **local bargaining**.
2) **Individual bargaining** means that employers can decide to pay an employee what they think he or she is worth to the firm. This can reduce wage bills and reward excellent staff. It also provides a financial incentive to the employee.
3) **Local bargaining** is where employees at an **individual workplace** bargain collectively. It's different from national collective bargaining by a trade union.
4) **Changes in the law** have weakened the power of unions, and allowed firms to move towards local and individual bargaining. **The state sector** has phased out some collective agreements.
5) Trade Union membership has **declined** (see p.47).

Pay Settlements must balance **Employer** and **Employee Needs**

Money (and the opportunity to earn more) **motivates** employees. As well as the actual wage, the relative wage is important — relative to other possible occupations, or the same occupation in a different part of the country. When people feel underpaid, their level of motivation falls.

1) Employers see wages as a **cost of production** that must be kept down — but not so low as to **demotivate** staff.
2) Employees see wages as a form of **financial recognition**, and therefore it's a motivator. It's also the ultimate determinant of their family's **standard of living**, and so ought to be high.

Employer/Employee Relations

Short Term Contracts and *Sub-contracting* provide *Employment Flexibility*

The labour needs of businesses vary **over time**. They may be working **close to full capacity** for some months and then **be less busy** a few months later. Businesses can deal with this by asking workers to work **overtime** to cover busy periods, and preventing them from working overtime during slack periods. There are other options as shown below:

Short-term contracts employ people for a short time

1) Short term contracts employ people for a **fixed period** of time (e.g. 6 months) and only re-employ them at the end of that period if **they are required**.
2) This may suit the employer but it **doesn't** meet the needs of **most** employees who prefer the certainty of a **secure**, **continuous** income.
3) Workers on **temporary** (short-term) contracts face the very real possibility of no renewal of contract (with no redundancy payments) at the end of the work period. This **weakens** their **bargaining power** — they'll feel they **need** to **cooperate fully** with the employer to increase the chances of contract renewal.
4) In addition, many of these workers are employed in ways that **aren't essential** for current production so if they threaten to go on **strike**, it won't have all that much **effect** on their employer.
5) In contrast, **permanent** staff have a **contract of employment** which establishes their duties and rights. This covers the circumstances (including redundancy pay) under which the contract can be terminated and the employee made redundant.
6) It's hard to build up a relationship with short term staff, and this can make communication difficult. Workers' social needs often aren't met by temporary work.

Sub-contracting means paying other firms to do some of the work

1) Sub-contracting means **paying other firms** for particular labour skills / services that others could do better, or for **occasional work** they couldn't **justify** employing **permanent** staff.
2) Examples of services that are often contracted out are company vehicle servicing and repair, computer **maintenance** and upgrading, office cleaning and canteen catering.
3) Many contractors are **sole traders** — self employed workers. They have to **negotiate** their **own rates of pay**.
4) Subcontracting can work out **cheaper** for the employer. They get a **trained** worker without having to spend money on **training**. Plus they don't have to pay **benefits** such as pension contributions.

Practice Questions

Q1 Describe the ways in which the needs of employers and employees (a) conflict, (b) match.

Q2 Explain the term "collective bargaining" and consider its merits.

Q3 How and why does local bargaining differ from collective bargaining?

Q4 Explain the meaning of the following terms, and identify the ways that a firm might benefit from them:
(a) introducing short-term contracts, (b) sub-contracting some activities.

Q5 Why are employees on short-term work contracts in a weaker bargaining position than permanent staff?

Q6 In what ways is the rate of pay a motivating factor for an employee?

Exam Question

Q1 Evaluate the advantages and disadvantages of collective bargaining to workers in a business with offices in Reading, Sunderland and Birmingham. (10 marks)

Don't even think about trying to collectively bargain with the examiners...

These pages aren't really that bad. The difference between collective and individual bargaining is fairly obvious — all you have to do is learn how collective bargaining is done, and what effects it has. Plus you have to know the ins and outs of short term contracts and subcontracting, and what the bargaining position of contractors is. So, get to learning it all.

Employee Participation

Remember, employees are stakeholders. If they're allowed and encouraged to participate in decisions that affect them, they are likely to be more motivated.

Employee Participation involves employees in Decision-Making

The work of mid 20th century **management theorists** such as Mayo, Maslow and Herzberg showed that **participation** could **motivate** workers. Before the 1950s, managers didn't see any need to involve employees in decision making. They believed that it was the boss's job to make decisions, and the worker's job to follow them.

Employee participation is also called **industrial democracy**. Ways businesses can **introduce participation** include:

Works councils or employee associations discuss work issues

1) Works councils are committees made up of employee representatives and employer representatives. Employee representatives are usually **elected**.
2) They **meet regularly** to discuss **general work issues** e.g. training, new technology and methods of work.
3) The sharing of ideas and information in a relatively **relaxed** atmosphere does a lot to improve **co-operation** between workers and management.
4) Where there's **no trade union presence** in a firm, works councils take care of **collective bargaining**.
5) **Quality circles** are like works councils, but they only discuss **quality** issues. They meet regularly to discuss ways of improving quality. Quality circles comprise of employees from **all levels** of the business.

Employee shareholders have more of a stake in the business

1) Employees can buy **shares** in the business. This gives them a higher **stake** in the business, and promises financial rewards in the form of dividends if the business performs well.
2) Shareholders can vote at the Annual General Meeting (AGM).
3) In practice, this one is actually more of a **financial motivator** than an instance of industrial democracy. There aren't usually enough employee shareholders to have any real influence at the AGM.

Employee directors have a seat on the board

1) Worker directors are **elected** by the employees. They serve on the **Board of Directors**.
2) **Employers** are sometimes **suspicious** of worker directors, believing that they may **spill board secrets** to the rest of the workforce.
3) **Unions** are also sometimes **suspicious** of worker directors. Unions worry that other workers will see the worker director as being on the **side of the bosses**.

Autonomous (independent) work groups give employees more control

1) Managers may **delegate** responsibility and give a team more **freedom to plan** and carry out their own work. This improves motivation.
2) Autonomous work groups may also be able to suggest **improvements** in **working practice**.
3) Some autonomous work groups **elect a leader**, and **appoint new staff**.
4) For this to work out, the **type** of work they're doing must be **suitable**, the group must **work well together** as a team, and they must have a good **blend** of skills.
5) Even then, it doesn't always work perfectly — some individuals may not want the **hassle** of deciding their own work plans.

Teamworking has practical Benefits and Problems

Teamworking = autonomous work groups.

Teamworking is when a business breaks down production into large chunks, each done by a **team**. In manufacturing, it's basically **cell production**, the alternative to production lines **division of labour**. Decisions are made by the team.

Benefits of teamworking:	Problems of teamworking:
It can motivate employees by making the job **less boring**.	Employees must be **multi-skilled**.
Decisions are made by **people in the team**.	Team members must **get on together**.
It can cut **management costs**, because it usually results in **delayering**.	**Experienced** middle managers are **lost**.
	Implementation is **expensive**.

Employee Participation

Employers can Encourage Participation and Involvement

Employees will participate **enthusiastically** in workplace discussion and decision-making under certain conditions.

- If they feel **valued**.
- If they feel their views are **listened to** and **taken into account** in the final decision.
- If they are treated **courteously**.

Firms can organise themselves in a way that **encourages** employees to feel respected and involved. This then leads to greater participation and commitment, which has some clear benefits for the firm.

1) Individual employees are more **highly motivated** to do their jobs well.
2) Employees might come up with good suggestions for **efficiency** improvements and **quality** improvements. This could help **improve productivity** and **product quality**.

Motivation and Participation go together

1) Under **Mayo's** theory of motivation, employee involvement satisfies an employee's need for **attention**.
2) Under **Maslow's** theory, employee participation and industrial democracy meet **social needs** and **self esteem** needs, and **can** go as far as meeting **self-actualisation** needs, as long as the employee feels that they can really **exercise control** over their own work and career.
3) Under **Herzberg's** theory, **hygiene factors** are met, and **dissatisfaction** factors such as poor company policy or poor working conditions are avoided or removed. Herzberg's **motivation factors** such as responsibility are increased.

Industrial Democracy has some Problems

In spite of the lovely **benefits** of industrial democracy, employee participation does create some **difficulties**.

1) It's **time consuming** and takes employees away from **immediate production**. This is especially critical if decisions need to be made **quickly**.
2) When industrial democracy **doesn't** produce the result that employees are looking for, it may worsen their attitude to the company.
3) Frequent **arguments** between employees, or between employer and employee could lead to personal animosity and worsen industrial relations.
4) Some employees just want to **get on with their job**, and react **negatively** to being invited to participate as they consider this an **intrusion** on their time.
5) Industrial democracy may mean that decisions are taken by a **half-informed group** rather than by the **relevant experts**.
6) Trade unions often **oppose** works councils and quality circles because they feel that employees should be using the union for help instead.

Practice Questions

Q1 How do (a) the employer, and (b) the employee benefit from increased industrial democracy?

Q2 What do works councils / employee associations do?

Q3 Why are autonomous work groups successful in some situations but not others?

Q4 How do Herzberg's hygiene factors and motivating factors relate to industrial democracy?

Exam Question

Q1 The proprietor of a chain of eight restaurants claims he has no need for participation schemes because he is "quite capable of making his own decisions". His staff are happy to get on with their jobs and do what they are told. Write a report relevant to his situation, outlining the benefits that greater employee participation might bring, AND explaining how he might go about introducing it into his business. (20 marks)

One machine, one vote...

"Industrial democracy" is a rather fancy and self-important name for the idea of having employees join in with the decision-making process. The key points to learn are all on these two pages — you have to know how employee participation is done, why it's good, and what problems can arise from it.

Trade Unions

About 7 million people in Britain belong to a trade union, which is about 25% of the total workforce. You might wonder why some people join trade unions while other people don't.

Trade Unions strengthen an employee's Bargaining Power

1) Trade unions act on behalf of **groups of employees** in the workforce when negotiating rates of **pay** and **working conditions** etc. with the employer.
2) By joining with others and belonging to a union an employee **strengthens** his or her **bargaining power** in a way that wouldn't be possible if he / she tried to bargain as an **individual** with the employer.

Trade Unions deal with much More than Pay Negotiations

Trade unions take action in the workplace

1) Trade unions **negotiate with employers** on behalf of their members to secure fair rates of pay and/or productivity bonuses for their work.
2) Trade unions help negotiate reasonable hours of **work**, and **paid holiday** entitlement.
3) Trade unions ask employers for **safe** and civilized **working conditions**.
4) Trade unions help their members get **job security** with protection against **mistreatment**, **discrimination** or **unfair dismissal**.

Trade unions take action at the national level

1) Trade unions **put pressure on the government** to introduce legislation that serves trade union interests.
2) The **minimum wage** was introduced in **1998** by the government after discussions with trade unions.
3) Trade unions pushed the government to make **redundancy payments** compulsory.
4) Trade unions ask for **pension protection** for those in private company pension schemes.

Trade unions take action in party politics

1) Many unions give **financial support** to the **Labour Party** because they think its policies represent their interests.
2) In the 1970s and 1980s, trade unions had a lot of power in the Labour Party. Since the **mid 1990s** they have **less power**.

Labour Party policy used to be decided by votes from members and "block votes" from unions — e.g. leaders of a trade union of 5000 people could decide to support a policy, and that policy would get all 5000 votes. In 1993, the Labour party stopped allowing union block votes, and policies were decided on a one member one vote basis.

Trade Unions are run by Local, Regional and National Officials

1) Local officials are called **shop stewards**. They're elected by employees.
2) Shop stewards represents the members on the workplace issues described above. The employer may allow shop stewards to use some time in work to carry out these union duties.
3) In **large** firms **several** shop stewards may be elected, each one representing a different group of employees. They usually come together as a **group** (**shop stewards' committee**) and negotiate with management this way.
4) When the issues are complex, shop stewards may request **help** from **regional officials**. These officials normally work **full time** for the union. They have a more detailed knowledge about employment law, bargaining procedures, economic pressures, etc.
5) The National Executive acts as the national spokesman for the union. It raises issues of concern with the **media** and **puts pressure on the government** to introduce reforms that would benefit their members.
6) The union's national executive is headed by an elected **General Secretary**.

Joint Consultation between Firm and Trade Union helps Prevent disputes

Many issues of difference between employers and trade unions **never** turn into a fully fledged **industrial dispute**. This is because the employer and the trade union reps **talk regularly** to sort things out **before** they get serious.

1) Joint consultation promotes a better **appreciation** of each other's **needs** and constraints.
2) It encourages a spirit of **co-operation** rather than confrontation.
3) Employers and union reps can **share ideas** for the benefit of everyone in the firm.

Trade Unions

There are **Different Types** of **Trade Unions**

Craft unions	Members of craft unions share a **common skill** but often work in **different locations.** Most of them started out as a traditional guild of craftsmen. Examples: Equity (the actors' union), the Writers' Guild of Great Britain, the PFA (Professional Footballers' Association).
Industrial unions	Members all work in the **same industry** but do a **wide range of jobs.** Their bargaining power is strong because strike action could bring production to a stop. Examples: RMT (the transport workers' union), NUM (National Union of Mineworkers).
General unions	Members range across **many different industries** in **many different occupations.** General unions tend to have a very **large number** of members. Examples: the GMB, the TGWU (Transport and General Workers Union).
White-collar unions	Members work in **administration** or **non-manual occupations.** In recent decades these unions have increased their membership, because of the growth in employment in these sectors. Examples: NUT (National Union of Teachers) and NUJ (National Union of Journalists).

Trade unions are particularly strong in **heavy industry** (e.g. mining, steelmaking) and **transport** (e.g. railways and ports). There's also strong union membership in the **public sector**, e.g. teachers, nurses and firemen.

Not all businesses **Recognise Trade Unions**

Many employers find it useful to negotiate through a trade union, so they're willing to **recognise trade unions** in the workplace.

Other employers prefer to **deal directly** with their employees. They either **don't recognise** trade unions, or **discourage** employees from joining a trade union. They consider unions to be **backward looking**, holding up innovation and improvements, and **preventing** managers from **managing effectively**.

There's been a **Decline** in **Union Membership** since the 1980s

The total number of people belonging to trade unions has **fallen** in recent years because:

1) Some industries that were **heavily unionised** have **reduced** their **output** and employment dramatically — e.g. coal mining, steelmaking, ship building.
2) Some employers, especially those in many of the newer service industries (call centres, leisure industry, retailing) have **discouraged staff from joining unions**. They prefer to discuss issues with an association made up of just their own employees.
3) **Government legislation** has **reduced** the **bargaining power** of the unions (see p.50) and some employers don't recognise unions, so the incentive for an employee to join is lower.

Practice Questions

Q1 Why is there a need for trade unions?

Q2 What do trade unions do for their members?

Q3 Would you join a trade union if you had a job with the opportunity to do so? Explain your answer.

Q4 How are trade unions organised?

Exam Question

Q1 Imagine you are the senior manager of a medium-sized clothes retailer employing 600 people with 10 stores spread across the country. Evaluate the two possible options below.
(1) Accept union recognition and encourage your staff to join,
OR (2) Resist union recognition and discourage your staff from joining. (8 marks)

You want a top tip — hang on, I'll have to talk to my union rep about that...

There's a fair old bit of detail on trade unions. It doesn't let up — there's more right up to page 51. But the basic facts on trade unions are here. You can be asked about the pros and cons of joining a union, and what unions do for workers. You might have to comment on union strength in a particular sector of industry, if it's relevant to a case study in the exams.

Industrial Disputes

Strikes, work to rule, overtime bans — they're all ways of putting pressure on employers.

Industrial Disputes happen when an Employer and Trade Union Can't Agree

1) Many conflicts appear on the surface to be a dispute over **wages** and **working conditions**. However, there may be **other grievances** caused by various human factors:
   - **Frustration** and **alienation** caused by **lack of communication** from managers or frequent **changes** in work practices.
   - **Stress** and **insecurity** caused by changing work patterns and **fears of redundancy**.
2) These feelings are difficult to express and quantify in argument — so it's often **easier** to turn the dispute into one about the more **usual workplace issues**.
3) Managers who **communicate effectively** and organise staff work responsibilities **consistently** will have a more **motivated workforce**, who'll be less likely to start a dispute.

Unions take Industrial Action — Work to Rule, Overtime Bans and Strikes

If the trade union fails to reach an agreement with the employer through negotiation, then they can apply more pressure by taking **industrial action** to reduce production. There are various tactics used, which gradually increase pressure.

1) **Work to rule** — employees stick 100% to the terms of their **contract**. They only do the tasks that their contract **specifically** asks them to do. This usually **slows production**.
2) **Go slow** — employees simply work more **slowly**.
3) A **ban on overtime** — exactly what it says. Employees don't work **overtime** when they're **asked** to. They don't come in early or work late or work at weekends.
4) **Strike** — employees withdraw their labour and **don't go to work**. This might be a **one-day strike** to **warn** the employer that they're serious about the issue, or a more **prolonged** strike.

Queen Victoria worked to rule, in her own way...

Industrial disputes have to be Resolved Eventually

A slow-down or stoppage of production means less output, sales and profit for the employer. It also means lower earnings for the employee. Because **both parties** are suffering they need to reach an agreement quickly. There's a clear incentive for both parties to return to negotiations.

In addition to the employer and employee, **other stakeholders** suffer from lost production.

1) Local businesses suffer from the **reduced spending** of those employees.
2) **Customers** can't get they goods or services they want.
3) Other firms may rely on this firm for their raw materials or components.
4) **The firm's suppliers** suffer, especially if the firm is an important customer.

Final Agreements reflect the Bargaining Strength of Both Sides

The final agreement / compromise reached reflects the relative bargaining strength of the union and the employer. This depends upon a variety of factors.

1) Whether there are **alternative** sources of **labour** and **production** (e.g. other factories in this country or abroad) that the employer could use.
2) When **stocks** of **finished products** are already available, a production stoppage is not so serious. The shelves will still be stocked, and **customers** won't even notice.
3) **Public opinion** is very important. An industrial dispute might harm the business' relationship with customers. Customers may **resent** either the union, or the employer, for failing to get things sorted out.
4) The **law** may constrain the actions that the union can take to reduce production.
5) The **size** of the firm is an issue — it may have **enough resources** to **cover** the loss of production and profit.

Industrial Disputes

Employers *and* ***Unions*** *often use* ***Other Organisations*** *to act as a* ***Mediator***

If the employer and union can't reach an agreement that **satisfies them both**, they might call on **another organisation** to act as **mediator** and / or **jury** to help resolve the dispute.

Industrial tribunal

This usually meets to deal with claims of **unfair dismissal** or **discrimination**. It hears the arguments of **both sides** and then announces its verdict. If it decides **against the employer** it may make them pay **compensation** to the employee.

ACAS — the Advisory, Conciliation and Arbitration Service

The Advisory, Conciliation and Arbitration Service does exactly what the name says.

1) **Conciliation** — ACAS **meets both parties** in the dispute, usually separately, and tries to develop **common ground** that they can both eventually accept.
2) **Arbitration** — It can appoint an **independent arbitrator** who considers the claims and declares what the outcome should be. If both sides agree, this outcome can be **legally binding**. There are two types of arbitration:
   - **Compromise arbitration** is a result which lies somewhere between what the employer wants, and what the employee wants. It sounds good, but there's a downside — it may encourage both **union** and **employer** to adopt **extreme** first demands in order to **bias** the eventual compromise towards their position.
   - **Pendulum arbitration** makes a simple choice for one or other of the competing claims — there's no compromise, and **no middle ground**. This encourages parties to adopt a more **reasonable** position to try to get the arbitrator to pick their side.

Employers *and* ***Employees*** *can* ***Reduce*** *the* ***Opportunity*** *for conflict*

1) **Single union agreement** or **single union recognition** only negotiates with one union. In one firm there may be **several unions**, each representing different employees. A large amount of management time is taken up in ensuring that any agreement with **one union** is **compatible** with the demands of all the others. The **single union agreement** avoids this because all negotiations are conducted with **just one recognised union**. This system is most likely to be introduced when a new firm is first established.
2) **No strike agreements** are where the employer provides an **independent system** for negotiating pay rises and working conditions in return for a **no-strike promise** from employees. This is more usual for some critical services such as the police force, where strikes would affect wider society.

Practice Questions

Q1 Explain why disputes may not always be about boring old pay and conditions.

Q2 List and describe the different kinds of industrial action a union might take in a dispute with an employer.

Q3 Explain who suffers in a dispute and why.

Q4 Explain the roles performed by the following: (a) industrial tribunal, (b) ACAS.

Q5 How do the following reduce the likelihood of disputes and production stoppages:
(a) Single union agreement / recognition? (b) No strike agreement?

Exam Questions

Q1 "Trade union members will lose more than they gain when they enter into a dispute with an employer." Evaluate this claim. (8 marks)

Q2 Consider a recent industrial dispute and analyse it in terms of the following: its causes, the tactics used by the union, the consequences for those affected, factors influencing the relative strengths of the two sides and the final settlement. (12 marks)

You poor students don't even get paid in the first place...

Industrial disputes have to be resolved before everything goes Pete Tong. It's not in the employees' best interests to be on strike for a long time — they lose pay, and damage their job prospects by damaging the industry. It's best to get things sorted ASAP. What you need to know is how disputes affect businesses and how they get resolved — tribunals, ACAS, etc.

Employment Law

Employment law regulates what employers, employees and trade unions can and can't do in their relationships with each other.

There are **Two** main areas of **Employment Law**

1) **Collective labour law** regulates the relationship between institutions (e.g. between firms and trade unions).
2) **Individual labour law** identifies the rights of the individual employee and their obligations to the employer.

Collective Labour Law controls what **Unions** can do

1) Unions can represent their members in discussions with the employer and ultimately call them out on strike, but this has to be done **within the law**.
2) During the **1980s** and **1990s**, the government passed a series of **laws** to control the way that **industrial relations** (negotiations between union and employer) were conducted.
3) At the time the government thought trade unions had **too much bargaining strength** in industrial relations. This pushed up **wage rates**, which in turn pushed up production costs and **prices**. This **wage and price inflation** made British goods **less competitive** in the global market.
4) The changes in the law reduced the bargaining power of unions. They're summarised **below**.

Employment Act 1980	Firms could **refuse to recognise** a union. Picketing was restricted to workers' **own place of work**.
Employment Act 1982	Trade unions could be sued. **Union-only clauses** were **banned**.
Trade Union Act 1984	Unions had to have a **secret ballot** before striking.
Employment Act 1988	Unions **couldn't punish** members who didn't strike.
Employment Act 1990	Employers could **sack** workers who went on **unofficial strike. Closed shop agreements** were **ended** — no one could be refused a job because they weren't in the right union.
Trade Union Reform and Employment Rights Act 1993	Unions had to give **7 days' notice** of a strike to employers. Secret ballots had to be done by **post**.

5) There's been a move away from "**voluntarism**" where an employer and the trade union(s) representing the employees at a particular workplace come up with an agreement that only applies to that workplace — e.g. not to strike, or to inform the employer a few days before a strike. Voluntary agreements have been **replaced** by the **collective labour laws** in the table above.

Individual Labour Law controls what rights **Employees** have

1) An employee has a legal right to **fair treatment** while at work, and also while looking for employment.
2) These anti-discrimination laws **prevent** employers from **acting unfairly**, and ensure fair treatment for individuals:

Equal Pay Act (1970)	A man and woman doing the **same** or an **equivalent** job should receive the **same rate of pay**. Followed up by EU Equal Pay Directive in 1975.
Sex Discrimination Act (1975)	A person cannot be discriminated against on grounds of **gender** or **marital status** for recruitment, promotion, training or dismissal.
Race Relations Act (1976)	A person cannot be discriminated against on grounds of **colour**, **race**, **national origin**, or **ethnic origin**.
Disability Discrimination Act (1995)	The employer must make efforts to ensure that **disabled people** can be employed in that place of work (e.g installing wheelchair ramps).

3) Anyone feeling **discriminated against** on the basis of sex, race or disability can go to an **industrial tribunal** (often set up by **ACAS**) to seek **compensation**. The tribunal listens to the arguments and makes a judgement.

The Data Protection Act gives **Employees** rights to privacy

Businesses hold **data** about their employees on **computer** — this includes things like their date of birth, address, and bank account details. Employees wouldn't want this information getting into the wrong hands.

The **Data Protection Act (1998)** says that anyone holding data about a person can't do anything with that data (e.g. pass it on to someone else) without the person's **consent**. Also, organisations can't pass on data if it's not **necessary**.

Employment Law

*Employees' **Pay** and **Working Conditions** are protected by the **Law***

1) Employees have the right to have a **contract of employment** setting out the **expected tasks** of the job.
2) They have the right to **protection** from **unfair dismissal**. (See Industrial Tribunals on p.49). Employees can be sacked for gross misconduct, or for failing to carry out duties. They can be made redundant if the job doesn't exist any more. Being dismissed for any other reason can be regarded as **unfair dismissal** and an employee can challenge the decision. This can be **costly** for a business.
3) Employees have the right to a **safe** working environment. The **Health and Safety at Work Act (1974)** states that the employer must ensure the working environment is safe. This covers a wide range of potential dangers: electrical equipment, hazardous substances and materials, moving machinery, etc. The firm can be fined if it fails to reach the minimum level required by the law.
4) Workers have the right to a certain number of **paid holidays** per year, plus public holidays. The **European Working Time Directive** sets out the entitlement as 4 weeks' paid leave per year.
5) Employees have the right to be **paid** on or above the **national minimum wage**.
6) They have the right to **confidentiality**, and can expect that the employer keeps their personal records private.
7) Employees have the right to **paid maternity** and **paternity** leave, and the right to **job security** while on maternity leave. **Mums** get 6 months' paid leave (not on full pay), and 6 months' unpaid, plus employers have to **hire a temp** to cover for the employee. This can be **expensive** for businesses — and it can sometimes be a source of **discrimination** against women. **Dads** get two weeks' paid paternity leave.

> **In return, the employee has obligations to their employer.**
> These include: **attendance** for work, **punctuality**, **willingness** to do and **complete** any **reasonable work** requested, **honesty** and **courtesy** to others. Any serious breach of these could lead to the employee being **disciplined** and ultimately **dismissed**.

8) All this employment legislation has an **impact** on businesses, mainly through **additional costs**.

European Union Law** has had an impact on **UK Industrial Relations

Britain's membership of the **European Union** means that EU directives apply in this country. The "Social Chapter" of the Maastricht Treaty (1992) included additional labour market regulations and employee rights.

1) The **Working Time Directive** of 1998 says employees need not work for more than **48 hours per week**, unless they **choose** to.
2) EU law gives **part time** and **full time** workers the **same** employment rights.

Labour Law** has an impact on the **Employer** in a **Global Market

1) A firm interested in profit wouldn't normally offer these protections for their employees off their own bat, because they push up **production costs** and **prices**, leading to **fewer sales**.
2) To maintain a **level playing field**, the law and European directives impose these obligations on all businesses so any firm which chooses to be nice to their employees isn't penalised.
3) However, now that competition is **global**, imposing these expensive obligations on only British and European firms may put them at a disadvantage when selling into world markets.

Practice Questions

Q1 Explain the terms: (a) collective labour laws, (b) individual labour laws.

Q2 In what ways has collective employment law reduced the power of trade unions?

Q3 How is the individual protected from discrimination in the labour market?

Q4 List five rights and five obligations that an employee has.

Exam Question

Q1 "An individual firm should be left free from legal interference to negotiate pay, working rights, and obligations with its own workforce." Evaluate the arguments behind this statement. (14 marks)

Now is not the time to go on strike...

There is an awful lot of law to learn on these pages. Don't be too faint of heart, though, because it's possible to learn it all. Tackle the Employment Acts first — make sure you know what unions could do before and after the Acts. Then take your individual labour law bits one at a time — discrimination, Data Protection, then working conditions, then pay. Not so bad.

Human Resource Management (HRM)

These pages tell you how businesses figure out their staff needs.

Human Resource Management looks after All Workers in a business

Human resources (HR) departments are **different** from traditional **personnel departments.** Personnel departments were concerned with just **hiring and firing**, HR departments do this and **keep supporting staff** in order to keep them **contributing** to the business. Human resource management (HRM) is **integrated** into the corporate planning of the business.

Workforce Planning is a key area of Human Resource Management

1) Human Resources plans for a firm's future staffing needs — **how many workers** will be needed and what kind of workforce will be needed — **skilled/unskilled**, **full-time/part-time**.
2) HRM plans how to **recruit** staff — where to advertise, how to interview etc.
3) Human Resources also decides how to treat staff while they're working for the business — how to **use their skills**, how to **retain** them, how to **train** and **reward** them, and eventually how to **terminate** their employment.
4) **Human Resources strategies** can be **short-term** (e.g. recruiting part-time staff for Christmas sales in retailing) or **long-term** (e.g. anticipating growth or a change in production techniques).

HRM departments in a business assess **demand for workers** in several ways:

1) HRM departments ask **other experienced managers** for their **opinion** and **advice**.
2) **Past statistics** (back data) are used to see if employee numbers have **risen**, **fallen** or **stayed the same.**
3) An increase or decrease in **demand for product** means an increase or decrease in **need for workers.**
4) Human Resources analyse the **current staff details** to see how many are likely to **leave** or **retire** in the near future.
5) The introduction of **new techniques** (automation etc.) will alter the number of workers needed.
6) HRM do an **internal stock take**. They look at all the **jobs** in the organisation — what each job entails and what sort of **qualities** and **skills** are needed. They see whether current staff **match** these requirements.

Human Resources also need to assess the potential **supply** of **new workers**:

1) They check the **level of unemployment** in the area to find out how many people are looking for work.
2) **Local infrastructure** is important — good housing, transport and schools can **tempt** people to the area.
3) HRM see how many **school and college leavers** are seeking employment locally.
4) HRM see if **competitors** are recruiting a similar workforce — if there'll be **competition** for workers.

Workforce Planning coordinates with Corporate Planning

1) Workforce plans have to **fit in** with the firm's other plans, and the overall **corporate plan**.
2) They must be coordinated with the **marketing plan** and the **production plan** — e.g. a plan to expand production and increase market share will require **more workers** and **new training**.
3) Changes in **production style** require **retraining**, **recruitment** and **redeploying** (moving workers to another job in the firm). Capital intensive production requires workers with fewer skills. Teamworking requires more skills.

Achieving Labour Targets means Expanding or Reducing the workforce

1) If a business thinks they need to **expand**, they have to decide whether to recruit **externally** (from outside) or **internally** (by training and promoting current employees).
2) **Reducing** the workforce is much harder than expanding the workforce.
3) The **least painful** method is through **natural wastage** — this is where staff leave of their own accord, by leaving for **other work** or through **retirement**, and aren't replaced.
4) If natural wastage isn't enough a firm may offer its older workers **early retirement** — a **financial encouragement** to retire early.
5) A business may need to make some of its workers **redundant** — they have to leave as their job won't exist any more. Under the **Employment Rights Act** of 1996, workers who've been with a business for a **year** have the right to **severance pay** (the actual amount depends on the length of service and the wage at the time of redundancy). Businesses **can't re-advertise** a redundant job — redundancy means the **job doesn't exist.**
6) The **Employment Protection Act** of 1978 protects workers against **unfair dismissal**. (See p.51).

Human Resource Management (HRM)

There are *Two* main *Approaches* to *Human Resource Management*

HRM can be '**hard**' or '**soft**'. Hard HRM acts a control technique whereas soft HRM focuses on staff development. The HRM approach a business adopts will depend on the **leadership styles** and attitudes towards staff within the business, which are often a reflection of its **organisational culture**.

Hard HRM

1) Employees are thought of as a **resource**, just like any other resource, e.g. machinery.
2) Employees are hired and fired on a **short-term basis**. So workers may have high levels of job insecurity.
3) Motivation is largely through pay, often related to performance.
4) Managers tend to be McGregor's **Theory X** managers and are often autocratic leaders.
5) Managers closely monitor worker performance and appraisals are **judgemental**.
6) Training is only done to meet **production** needs.
7) Jobs are designed to **maximise productivity**, even if it means creating jobs that involve dull, repetitive tasks.
8) It is based on ideas developed from Taylor's **scientific management**. Taylor believed that if employees were left to their own devices they would do the minimum amount of work possible.
9) Hard HRM can be very **demotivational** for the workforce. Boring, repetitive jobs can make employees feel **undervalued**. Employees are unlikely to use their initiative or be very flexible.
10) Employees are unlikely to be committed or loyal to the organisation, which can cause **high levels** of **staff turnover**.

Soft HRM

1) Employees are seen as the **most important** resource.
2) Employees are managed on a **long-term basis**.
3) Motivation is through **empowerment** and **development**. **Communication** and collaboration are also important.
4) Managers tend to be **Theory Y** managers and take a democratic approach.
5) Appraisals are **developmental**, focusing on how the employee can improve in future.
6) Training is done to meet **development** needs and to develop potential.
7) It encourages **commitment** and good performance from workers. Employees are encouraged to believe that they are individually helping to contribute towards the overall business objectives.
8) It's based on the work of Maslow, Mayo and Herzberg, who identified the importance of **fulfilling employees needs**.
9) It can be an **expensive** and **time consuming** approach.
10) Once employees have completed all the training they want they might leave for a better job.

Practice Questions

Q1 Why must workforce planning coordinate with corporate planning?

Q2 What is redundancy?

Q3 Theory Y managers tend to use which type of human resource management?

Q4 What are disadvantages of adopting a hard HRM approach?

Exam Question

Q1 What would the HR department of a supermarket need to consider when carrying out workforce planning? (8 marks)

It's a tough job, but someone's got to do it...

For employees, a soft HRM approach can seem by far the better option. For employees, soft HRM means training, job security and not getting shouted at so much. But from a business's point of view soft HRM can be expensive and time-consuming. If a business needs to increase productivity, they may decide to use a hard HRM approach.

Methods of Reward

*Most working people in the UK get paid a monthly **salary** or a weekly **wage**. There are other kinds of financial motivation, like commission and fringe benefits.*

Time Based Payment gives an Hourly or Weekly Wage

1) Workers who are paid a **weekly wage** get a set rate of so many **pounds per hour**. The more hours they work the more they get paid. There's a minimum wage — in 2005 this was £5.05 per hour for adults over 22. Workers usually work a **fixed working week** of about 40 hours, and get paid more for each hour of **overtime** they work.
2) Workers who get paid a monthly **salary** get so many **thousand pounds a year**, divided into 12 monthly payments. The salary isn't directly related to the number of hours worked — salaried employees work a minimum number of hours a week, and then as many hours as it takes to get the job done.

Production Based payment pays either a Piece Rate or Commission

1) Some **production workers** are paid by **piece rate** (or piece work) — they get paid so many pounds or pence **per finished item**. The more the worker produces, the more they get paid.
2) Sales people are usually paid **commission** — a **percentage** of the **sales** they achieve. Most sales staff get a low **basic salary** and earn commission on top of that, but some get commission only.
3) Workers can be paid a **bonus** or a **higher rate of pay** if they achieve above a **target** rate of productivity.

Performance Based payment gives More to employees who Meet Targets

1) **Performance related pay (PRP)** gives more money to employees who meet their targets.
2) Performance related pay is linked in with employee **appraisals**. Appraisal is the process of evaluating the **development** and **performance** of an employee.
3) Appraisals can be done by **interview**, or by measuring productivity at regular intervals.
4) Some employees worry that they won't get a performance related pay rise if they don't **get on** particularly well with the manager doing the appraisal interviews.

> 1) Employee appraisal has two sides — it can look for ways to **help** an employee **improve**, or it can **judge** an employee to see if they're **good enough**.
> 2) Appraisal was traditionally about checking employee **skill** and **productivity**, giving **pay rises** to good employees and **pay cuts** (or the sack) to lousy ones.
> 3) Modern appraisal is a combination of **employee development** and reward adjustment — it's linked to **both** training and pay.
> 4) The type of appraisal used depends on **leadership style**. **Autocrats** favour **judgemental appraisal** and **democrats** favour **developmental appraisal**.

Businesses also Reward Employees with other Benefits

Julia valued fringe benefits.

1) In addition to their weekly / monthly pay, employees may also get **fringe benefits**.
2) These include **staff discount** for company products (very common in retail), employer contributions to employee **pensions**, private **medical insurance**, health club membership, a company **car**, **profit sharing** schemes and options to buy **shares** in the company.
3) These are all **financial** rewards — they're things that can be objectively valued in terms of money. It'd cost the employees money to buy their own health insurance, gym membership etc.
4) Don't forget the impact of **non-financial** rewards such as praise, training, or additional responsibility.
5) Most financial benefits are liable for income tax — they're taxed on their "cash equivalent" which is the price it'd cost to buy them. Most benefits can't be used as a tax loophole — a way of paying someone money without them paying tax on it. However, employees don't have to pay tax on pension scheme contributions or share options of less than about £3000.

Methods of Reward

Training and *Development* is a *Reward In Itself*

1) Training helps the employee to be **good** at their job. It's in the interests of the employer to train the employee to be as productive as possible.
2) Training **fulfils employee needs**. It meets Mayo's attention need, Maslow's self-esteem and self-actualisation needs, and it's one of Herzberg's motivating factors.
3) **All employees** need training, not just new employees.
4) Businesses need to build training into their **workforce plan**. They must assess when employees are likely to **need** training. This could be because of **reorganising** production or making a new product which required new assembly skills.
5) There could also be a need for training to help an employee **develop**, to prevent them from getting **bored** in their job, and to allow them to take **new responsibility**.
6) Businesses should **evaluate** their training to see how it's **working** — using clear, measurable objectives. Managers should be able to compare **training costs** with the **financial gains** from improved performance.
7) Sometimes businesses might not want to be the **best** at training staff. They worry that **competitors** will "**poach**" the staff they've trained. If all businesses avoided training staff because they don't want them to be poached, there'd be **no training,** which would **severely affect the labour** market.

Employee Development aims to make employees *Fulfilled and Motivated*

1) Some organisations do **employee development** as well as training.
2) Whereas training focuses on skills needed for **specific job tasks**, development programmes try to help employees learn and improve **broader** skills such as people management, budget setting or customer service. Employee development helps employees take on new responsibility and **get ahead** in the organisation — so it can be quite highly motivating.
3) The idea is that the organisation will benefit from a more broadly skilled, **fulfilled** and **motivated** employee.

Reward Schemes must fit the organisation's *HRM Style*

1) **Money** is the main reward in a **hard HRM** approach. Basic pay may be low, but workers will be rewarded for **performance** through commission or bonuses.
2) With **hard HRM**, rewards will probably be based on workers meeting specific **targets** or **objectives**.
3) With **hard HRM** other types of rewards, like **training** and employee development, will be considered a **waste**.
4) Soft HRM businesses won't ignore financial rewards but money will only be one of a number of different rewards on offer.
5) **Training** and **development** is a major reward with **soft HRM**, because worker development is an important aim of soft HRM.
6) Other rewards with **soft HRM** will **encourage** workers to **commit** to the business for the long term, e.g. offering a pension.

Practice Questions

Q1 Give three examples of fringe benefits.

Q2 Give two types of rewards a business with a soft HRM approach would offer.

Exam Question

Q1 There is a shortage of postmen in London. The Royal Mail could resolve this shortage in two ways. It could increase the pay for all postmen across the whole country or it could restrict wage rises so that they apply to London staff only. Evaluate the impact of these choices on each of the following:

a) Royal Mail (production costs, recruitment, motivation, etc). (6 marks)

b) Employees of Royal Mail (postmen and others). (6 marks)

Pay a basic wage of peanuts and give bananas as bonuses, get motivated monkeys...

There's quite a lot more detail on reward schemes in A2 Business Studies compared to AS. You're expected to know how payment and reward tie in with appraisal and employee management. They're particularly keen on getting you to say how HRM fits in with the activities and objectives of a business — why they might want to train staff, why they might not, etc.

Measuring Labour Effectiveness

A business needs to measure the effectiveness of every resource used, including the workforce. Managers can use qualitative data and numerical ratios to assess the ***efficiency*** *and* ***competitiveness*** *of a workforce.*

Labour Productivity measures How Much each Employee Produces

$$\text{Labour Productivity} = \frac{\text{Output per period}}{\text{Number of employees}}$$

Example: A factory has 30 workers per shift working 3 shifts per day to produce 9000 DVD players per week.
Productivity = 9000 ÷ 90 workers = **100** DVD players per worker per week.

The **higher** the labour productivity, the **better** the workforce is performing. As labour productivity **increases**, labour costs per unit **fall**. This is important in **labour intensive** firms, where labour costs are a high proportion of total costs.

Ways to improve labour productivity

1) Labour productivity can be improved by **improving worker motivation.**
2) Training can make workers more productive.
3) Labour productivity can also be improved by changing to **more efficient** methods of production — e.g. changing from job to batch production or from batch to flow production. These gains need to be balanced against the **costs** of changing production method, and the **reduced production flexibility.**
4) Improvements can be had by **rewarding** increased productivity. Paying workers using a **piece-rate** system encourages staff to produce more. Managers should take care that **quality** doesn't suffer in the process.

1) Increasing labour productivity means **redundancies** and **job losses** unless sales increase. Businesses need to **plan** for the consequences of improved productivity to avoid upsetting staff.
2) Businesses should **monitor** their labour productivity over time. When they're setting targets, they should compare their productivity to **competitors' productivity** through **benchmarking**.
3) Businesses must **balance** productivity against issues such as product **quality** and long-term worker **motivation**.

Absenteeism measures the Proportion of Time employees are Off Work

$$\text{Absenteeism} = \frac{\text{Number of staff days lost}}{\text{Number of days}} \times 100$$

1) Absenteeism is measured as a percentage. Obviously, **low** is best.
2) Figures need to be analysed in the **context** of each industry. For example, **police** officers might have **higher** than average figures because of the dangers and stresses of the job, while **sales** people paid on commission have **lower** rates because time off work can reduce their pay.
3) **Causes** of absenteeism include poor **working conditions**, poor **relationships** with managers and other staff, **stress** or **disillusionment** with the job, and poor **motivation**.
4) Absenteeism **increases costs**. It results in **lost opportunities**, e.g. sales enquiries left unanswered. There's also a cost of additional **wages** to cover for the absent employee — this is often expensive **overtime** pay.
5) Absenteeism increases if employees believe the firm **accepts** it as unavoidable. Some businesses require employees to fill in a **self-certification form** if they take any time off sick. Some require a **doctor's note** for anything over 7 days in a row off sick. **HR** or line managers may **interview** absent employees on their return to work to find out why they've been absent, and to let them know that their absenteeism has been noted.
6) There are several ways a firm might **reduce absenteeism**, depending upon what's causing it.

Method	How it works
Job enrichment	Employees with satisfying, challenging jobs **enjoy work** more than those with boring jobs, so they're less likely to miss work.
Improved relationships	Making employees feel **valued** will encourage them to be more **loyal** to their employers and reduce absenteeism rates.
Improved conditions	Good working conditions reduce **work-related illness** and **injury** — e.g. ergonomically designed workstations reduce RSI.
Flexi-time	This stops many employees missing work due to **family commitments** or **medical appointments.**

Measuring Labour Effectiveness

Labour Turnover measures the Proportion of Staff who Leave each year

$$\text{Labour Turnover} = \frac{\text{Number of staff leaving}}{\text{Average number of staff employed}} \times 100$$

Work out the part timers as if they were fractions of a full time employee. Two people who each work half a week = one person working a whole week.

Example: A business has 100 full time staff and 100 part-time staff who each work 50% of a normal week. Over a year 10 full time and 10 part-time staff leave.

Average staff = 100 + (100 × 0.5) = **150**. **Average leaving** = 10 + (10 × 0.5) = **15**, so **labour turnover** = 15÷150 = **10%**.

1) The **higher** the figure the larger the proportion of workers leaving the firm each year.
2) **External causes** of high labour turnover include changes in regional **unemployment** levels, and the growth of other local firms using staff with **similar skills**.
3) **Internal causes** of high labour turnover include poor motivation of staff, low wages, and a lack of opportunities for promotion. Staff will **join other firms** to increase their pay and job responsibilities.
4) A **poor recruitment** process which selects poor candidates will also increase labour turnover.
5) Increased **delegation**, **job enrichment**, higher **wages** and better **training** can reduce employee turnover.
6) Businesses need **some** labour turnover to bring new ideas in. Labour turnover of 0 means no one **ever** leaves.
7) Businesses can use the labour turnover figures to help them develop their HR strategy. For example, a high turnover rate could mean a business needs to introduce measures to keep staff for longer.

Benefits of high staff turnover	**Disadvantages of high staff turnover**
Constant stream of **new ideas** through new staff.	Lack of **loyal** and **experienced** staff who know the business.
Firm can recruit staff who've **already been trained** by competitors — saves money.	Firm **loses** staff it has **trained**, often to direct competitors.
If sales fall, firm can reduce workforce through **natural wastage** rather than costly redundancy.	**Training costs money** and **productivity drops** while new staff get trained.
Enthusiasm of new staff influences other workers.	**Recruitment** costs are high.

Health & Safety measures Time Lost through Accidents at work

$$\text{Health \& Safety} = \frac{\text{Number of staff days lost through work accidents}}{\text{Number of working days}} \times 100$$

1) Low numbers are **best**.
2) A work environment that's perceived as **dangerous** will damage employee **morale**. A high rate of absence due to work related injuries and illness causes bad publicity. Employees may seek **compensation** for accidents at work.
3) Many accidents at work are **avoidable**, so businesses can take action to make the workplace safer.
4) Some industries are more prone than others to accidents so firms should **benchmark** within their own industry.
5) Managers should compare this measure to calculations in **previous years** and also to the **absenteeism measure**.

Practice Questions

Q1 Define labour turnover.

Q2 State two possible causes of a high labour absenteeism measure.

Q3 What's the formula firms use to measure labour productivity?

Q4 State two benefits and two drawbacks of a high labour turnover percentage.

Exam Questions

Q1 Why should a major employer such as the NHS be concerned about differing absenteeism percentages in different hospitals, and what action might they take? (10 marks)

Q2 What problems might arise when changing the method of production to improve labour productivity? (6 marks)

How about a nice apple turnover... and custard...

Managers need to choose the right measures to focus on. For each one, there are good points and bad points of it being high, and good points and bad points of it being low. Remember that when you revise these measures — for the best marks, you need to put the facts into the context of the business. Focusing on absenteeism will suit some firms, but not others.

Research and Development

Businesses need to do technical research before launching new products.

Research and Development comes up with New ideas, products, and processes

1) Research and Development (R&D) does **technical research** to come up with new products and production processes. The idea is to design new processes that increase productive efficiency or to design new products that increase sales.
2) Coming up with new ideas is called **innovation**.
3) R&D is **related** to market research, but they're not the same. Market research **discovers** consumers' wants and R&D comes up with new products to **meet** customer wants.
4) R&D is the first step in a new product's life cycle. The most successful businesses have a **large portfolio** of products, **balanced** between **innovative new products** and proven older products, so they develop new products or plan modifications to existing products all the time.
5) Investment in R&D is important to ensure competitive advantage. The ability to launch a new product in the market is of great value. A business can charge a high price for its innovative product (this is called market skimming), and the product can achieve a sound **market image**, before competitors enter the market with **similar products** at **competitive prices**. The Sony Walkman is a great example of this.
6) Some industries are particularly **fast moving**, and need to **constantly** develop new products — e.g. the pharmaceutical industry, the microchip industry and the mobile telecommunications industry.

Research and Development is Costly and Risky but Essential

1) Research and Development is a very **costly** process.
2) It's also a **risky** process — it's estimated that in the **pharmaceutical** industry, only **one in twelve** new drugs **researched** are actually **developed** as having a commercial potential.
3) R&D turns raw ideas into **actual products**, or **actual new processes**. This can take a **long time**. Pharmaceutical R&D takes a very long time because new drugs must be rigorously tested before they can be used on people.
4) R&D is important in helping to develop **product quality**.
5) Some organisations choose not to have a specific R&D department, but instead to **adapt** and **modify** new products brought out by their **rivals**. This may be because the business is **risk averse**, or because its shareholders prefer profits to be paid as dividends in the short term rather than invested for the long term.
6) However, market leaders normally invest in R&D. They may do all their research in their **own R&D department**, or they may **buy in research** from **university** science and engineering departments.
7) **UK businesses** are often criticised for **not spending enough** on R&D.

1) Innovation is protected by **patents**. Patents are granted by the **Patent Office**, a government agency that checks that an invention is an **original** design.
2) The **holder** of a patent has the right to be the **sole manufacturer** of a **product** or **sole user** of a **process** for **20 years** after the patent is registered.
3) The holder of a patent can **sell** the right to use the patented process or make the patented product.

R&D can be classified as Pure, Applied or Development

1) **Pure research** is original scientific and technological research that **doesn't** have a **business application** in mind. The aim of pure research is to **understand** the science or technology **better** — pure research can be necessary to find out just what's possible, or to come up with a really exciting innovation. Pure research is usually done in science and engineering labs.
2) **Applied research** is original scientific and technological research with a **business application** in mind. The aim of applied research is to use science or technology to find a **good way of doing something**. This may be done in science and engineering labs, or in a firm's own R&D labs.
3) Development is linked to a specific product or system. It's all the work that's needed to develop a new or improved product or system.
4) Pure and applied research are usually written off as an **expense** on the profit and loss account. They're seen as **revenue expenditure** — a cost of doing business.
5) **Development costs** associated with a **particular project** may be treated as **capital expenditure**. This would mean including them on the balance sheet as an **asset**, and **depreciating** them over a number of years.

Research and Development

New Product Development (NPD) has Six Stages from Idea to Launch

1) Idea

The business comes up with **new ideas**, explores and **develops existing ideas** or **modifies competitors' ideas**. New ideas can come from **brainstorming** in a group, from **employee suggestions** or from **R&D department meetings**. New ideas are also discovered through **market research** finding out what consumers want, or from customers submitting requests to a business. Businesses can also use **already patented ideas**, for a fee.

2) Analysis and Screening

The business wants to see if the product can be produced and sold at a **profit**. All aspects of the idea are investigated — whether there's a **potential market** for it or not based on market research, whether the **technology** and **resources** exist to develop it, whether a **competitor** has an existing patent on a similar idea. At this stage, a **prototype** may be made to see what the product will be like.

3) Development

The **R&D department** develop a **working prototype**. They test it **scientifically**, and tweak the product design to make the **functional** design (how it works) and **aesthetic** design (how it looks, feels — or smells and tastes if it's a food) as good as possible. This is the real "meat" of research and development.

4) Value Analysis

The business tries to make the product good **value** for money. They look at the economy of **making**, **warehousing** and **distributing** the product to make sure the whole process will be **efficient** and value for money — for the **business**, and for the **consumer**.

5) Test Marketing ⟸ This is where the marketing department gets involved again.

The business sometimes sells the new product in a **limited geographical area**, and then analyses **consumer feedback** on the product, price and packaging. This allows **modifications** to be made before a wider launch.

6) Launch

All systems are go. A successful launch needs **enough stock** of the product to be distributed across the market, and an effective **promotion campaign** in place to **persuade** retailers and consumers to buy the product.

Time Based Competition means R&D should be as Fast as possible

1) **Intense international competition** means that many businesses feel they need to come up with new, better products, **all the time**. Businesses need to pursue **new product R&D** to maintain or increase their market share.
2) This increasing pressure has shifted the emphasis in product development from **price** and **quality** (**value analysis**) to **time based competition** — where the aim is to be the **fastest**. NPD is squeezed into the shortest time possible.
3) **Technology** also **changes rapidly**, so manufacturers are under pressure to develop products which are more modern and technologically advanced all the time. Computer **software** is often released before it's **really 100% ready**, and the software producer supplements the release with "**patches**" which fix any problems with the original release. This is because of **intense time pressure**.

Practice Questions

Q1 What's meant by "research and development"?

Q2 Give a reason why R&D is risky.

Q3 What is the difference between pure and applied research?

Q4 What's the link between R&D and product design?

Exam Question

Q1 Explain why it is important for a food manufacturer to invest in research and development. (10 marks)

They could be researching a new, tougher exam — just you watch out...

Hey, all those amazing new products have to come from somewhere. Just think, there are research and development eggheads beavering away even now, as we speak, to come up with something utterly amazing that we'll all rush out to buy. Of course, it could turn out to be yet another shampoo for colour treated hair, or yet another web publishing tool.

Critical Path Analysis

Critical Path Analysis is used to find the most cost-effective way of doing a complex project.

Critical Path Analysis works out the Quickest Way to Finish a Set Of Tasks

Critical Path Analysis (CPA) identifies the most **efficient** and **cost effective** way of completing a complex project — i.e. a project made up of a series of activities.

1) The various activities which together will make up the project are **identified**, and the **order** or **sequence** of these activities are identified.
2) The **duration** or how long each activity will take is **estimated**.
3) These factors are then arranged as a **network** or graph, showing the whole project from start to finish, and showing which tasks can happen at the same time.

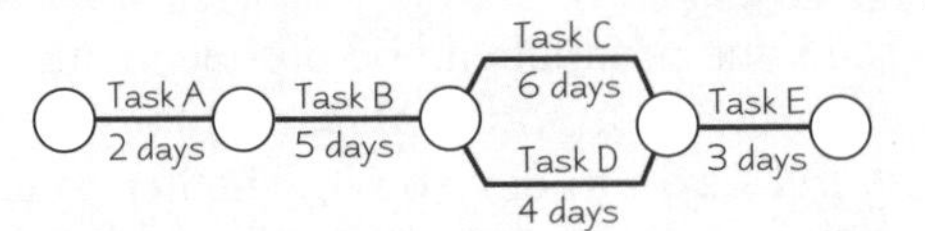

For large, complicated projects made up of lots of steps, computer programs are used to construct the network.

Task C and task D can be done at the same time.

4) The **shortest time** required to get from start to finish is identified. The sequence of tasks which have to be done one after another with **no gaps in between**, to get the project done as fast as possible, is called the **Critical Path**. Activities on the critical path are called **critical activities** — if they're delayed, the **whole project** is delayed.

Critical Paths include Earliest Start Times and Latest Finishing Times

1) Before and after each task on the CPA diagram there is a **node**, which shows the earliest start time (EST) for a task on a project and also the latest finishing time (LFT) for a task on the project.
2) **EST = earliest start time**. It tells you the **earliest possible day** of the project that you would be able to **start a task** on. You need to know this because there will be certain tasks in a project that can't be started until other tasks have been completed — e.g. you can't ice a cake before it's baked. Starting at the first node the EST is worked out by **adding** the **duration of the latest task** to the **EST in the previous node**.
3) **LFT = latest finishing time**. It's basically the **latest** time a task can be completed without **holding up** the **next activity** in the process. You work out the LFTs by **working backwards** from the **end** of the project — it's calculated by **subtracting** the **duration** of the task from the **LFT** of the **last task**.
4) **LFT** and **EST** are written on the right hand half of each **node**. The number on the left hand side is just the number of the node — the nodes are numbered left to right.

Number of node. — 3 | 7 / 7 — Earliest start time of next activity. / Latest finish time of last activity.

5) Some tasks will have **float time**, which is spare time available for a task. There are two ways of calculating float time:
   i) **Total float time** is the amount of spare time between the time an activity takes, and the time it must be completed by.
   LFT (this activity) – **Duration** (this activity) – **EST** (this activity) = **Float time**
   Example: 12 days LFT – **7 days** duration – **3 days** start time = **2 days float time.**
   ii) **Free float** is the difference between the time a task takes and the time where the **next task** has to start.
   EST (of the **next** activity) – **Duration** of task – **EST** (of **this** activity) = **Free float.**

Note: activities on the Critical Path don't have any float time.

Here's an Example of Critical Path Analysis

1) The project is made up of **eight separate tasks** A to H. Task **A** takes **4 days**, **B** takes **7 days**, **C** takes **9 days**, **D** takes **6 days**, **E** takes **5 days**, **F** takes **5** days, **G** takes **7** and task **H** takes **3 days**. Tasks B and C can be done at the same time. Task E can be done at the same time as D. Task F can be started at the same time as task A. Task G must be finished before H can begin. The network looks like this:

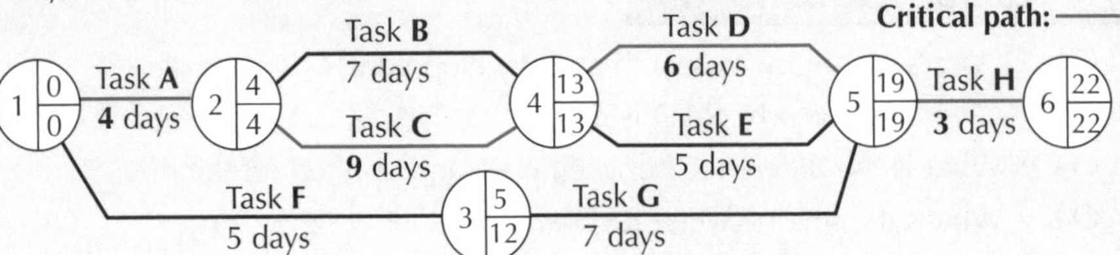

2) You can work out the **ESTs** of all the tasks by working **forwards** from the start of the project, and then work out the **LFTs** of the tasks by working backwards from the end of the project.
3) In each node on the critical path, the EST equals the LFT. Node 3 is off the critical path, and the EST and LFT are different — the EST of task G is 5 days after the start of the project and the LFT of task F is worked out by subtracting the duration of task G from the LFT of task G (19 days – 7 days = 12 days).
4) The **critical path** is task **A** followed by task **C**, then task **D, then** task **H**. Adding up the durations of these tasks tells you the project takes **22 days** in total — the EST and LFT in the final node are both 22 days.
5) **Task B** has a **float time** of **2 days** and **task E** which runs alongside **task D** has a **float time** of **1 day**.

Critical Path Analysis

Critical Path Analysis has several *Advantages*

1) CPA identifies the **critical activities** (activities on the critical path), which need to be supervised closely, to make sure they meet their deadlines.
2) Labour resources can be transferred from activities with **float time** to **critical activities**, to make sure that deadlines are met.
3) CPA allows managers to operate **Just-In-Time** production. **Resources** such as raw materials, labour and equipment can be employed right at the **earliest start time**, instead of hanging around waiting to be needed. This saves on the **storage costs** and opportunity costs of stock holding, and **improves liquidity**.
4) Critical path analysis helps firms forecast their **cash flow** — it gives definite earliest start times when cash will need to be spent on raw materials, which allows the firm to predict its liquidity.
5) Critical path analysis finds the shortest time possible for completing a complex project. This can give a competitive advantage. It's an important element of **time-based management**.
6) It's an excellent **visual aid** to communications, because it shows at a glance which steps take place at the **same time**, and which have any **float time**.
7) Critical path analysis forces managers to think about the activities involved in the project. Without the systematic approach of critical path analysis, something might be forgotten.
8) CPA can be used to review progress on individual tasks. If there are changes and modifications to the progress of the project, the critical path can be **updated** as the project goes on.

Critical Path Analysis has *Disadvantages* as well

1) Critical path analysis relies on **estimates** of how long each task will take. If these aren't accurate, the whole analysis will be inaccurate.
2) Unless **critical activities** are identified and supervised closely, there'll be **delays** to the whole project. Critical path analysis puts **pressure** on managers to **manage effectively** and **meet deadlines**.
3) Managers must make changes to the CPA once they know that delays are likely. Otherwise, it'll be inaccurate.
4) Constructing the CPA will require a significant amount of **planning** and **time**.
5) Critical path analysis sets **tight deadlines**, especially for critical activities. It's tempting for employees to **cut corners** in the rush to meet deadlines. **Quality** can suffer.
6) Critical path analysis can't tell you anything about **costs** — or anything about **how good** the project is.

Practice Questions

Q1 What do the initials EST and LST mean?

Q2 Explain the term "total float time".

Q3 What is meant by the expression "critical path"?

Q4 Give two advantages to managers of using critical path analysis.

Exam Questions

Q1 A project is analysed and six separate activities are identified. Activity A must be done first, and it has an estimated duration of 8 days. Activities B, C and D can take place at the same time — B takes 4 days, C 6 days and D 4 days. E is a separate activity and will take 7 days. F and G can take place at the same time — F taking 3 days and G five days.

Construct a critical path analysis from this data. Mark in the critical path and state the minimum number of days the project will take to complete. Answer on p.98. (8 marks)

Q2 What is the purpose of a critical path analysis? Provide and explain three advantages and three disadvantages of employing such a technique. (14 marks)

What did the critical path say — "get your badly dressed self off my gravel"...

To be honest, this is hard to learn from scratch. Once you've got a diagram to show the order of tasks in a project, and which ones can be done simultaneously, you can figure out where in the project there's spare time. Remember that you work out EST by working forwards from the start date, and you work out LFT by going backwards from the end date.

Controlling Operations

IT is used to plan and control operations. IT makes decision making easier and speeds up communication. Hooray for computers.

*IT is used to **Control Operations***

IT (Information Technology) has dramatically changed the way that businesses are run. It is now used in most parts of a business, but especially in the following areas:

1) **Production**
2) **Communication**
3) **Finance**
4) **Employment** and **Location**

Information management is **vital** to good decision making and operational control.
As IT is used more and more in business, the amount of **information available** to managers increases.
It's important to **manage** this information so that managers get the information they **need**, no more, no less.
Successful organisations keep **up-to-date** with changing information.

*IT helps make **Stock Control** more **Efficient***

1) Computers make **stock control** easier. Holding stock information in a database makes it much easier to monitor when new stocks are required.
2) Good computer links with suppliers make it easier to use a **Just In Time** system.
3) In retailing this is often combined with **Electronic Point of Sale** (**EPOS**) systems that rely on **barcodes** to record which products are being purchased by customers. This means stocks can be re-ordered automatically.
4) **Purchasing** over the Internet allows businesses to see at a glance which suppliers have the best prices. This cuts costs and speeds up purchasing.

*IT helps make **Production** more **Efficient***

1) **Computer-aided design** (CAD) uses computers to design new products, or make alterations to existing products. CAD produces 3D mockups on screen — managers don't have to wait for a **prototype** to be built before they know what the product will look like. This reduces the **time** and **cost** of product design.
2) **Computer-aided manufacture** (CAM) uses computers to produce a product, usually involving **robots** or computer numerically controlled machines (CNC). CAM is often combined with the CAD process — products are designed on computer, and the design data fed straight into the production machine. This is called **CAD/CAM**.
3) CAD and CAM can be used as part of a **flexible manufacturing system**. Businesses can **adapt** designs to meet the needs of **individual customers**.
4) **Manufacturing resource planning** (MRP II) software provides a computer model of the whole production process. It uses sales **forecast data** to draw up **purchasing requirements** for parts, and it comes up with a **production schedule** for all the business's orders that tries to maximise capacity utilisation.
5) With MRP II software, it's possible to see all the resources that will be used in production, before production starts. This allows managers to **see potential problems** and take **pre-emptive action** to sort them out. Managers can use the software to **predict** what would happen if they increased output by 2% or whatever amount.

*IT helps make **Communication Faster** and more **Effective***

Communication now happens very **quickly** thanks to IT. Information can be passed **between departments**, between businesses, and between businesses and their **customers** using fax, email and Internet. Storing information about customers on a database enables businesses to **personalise** their communication with customers.

1) Email is a fast and efficient method of communicating, both internally and externally.
2) The **Internet** allows businesses to reach a **larger customer base**, and do business **24 hours a day**. Customers can check a business's **webpage** for information rather than phoning a helpline or sending a letter in the post.
3) Businesses can set up **permanent data links** between departments and between sites. This allows up-to date information to be transferred instantly from one part of the business to another.
4) Businesses can use IT to **collect information** about their customers. **Store loyalty cards** collect information about what products customers buy, which can be used to **target special offers** to individual customers. **Online retailers** can **recommend** books or CDs that you might like, based on what you've bought from them before (this requires a large database and some expert human input).

Controlling Operations

IT helps make **Finance** departments more **Efficient**

Most businesses keep their **financial information** on **computers**. They use computer **software** to produce **budgets**, handle **payments** to suppliers and run their employee **payroll**.

1) **IT** helps with **budgetary control** and **variance calculation**. Once budgets have been set, the finance department can easily compare current expenditure levels with original budgets using **spreadsheets**.
2) **IT** helps with **forecasting and planning**. Large amounts of **data** can be held on computer, to make forecasting easier. Spreadsheets are used to calculate cash flow forecasts.
3) Computers are also used to **model complex financial planning tools** such as Internal Rate of Return (see p.36).
4) Spreadsheets allow managers to investigate "what if?" scenarios. They can see the impact of **potential changes** in expenditure or sales at the proverbial **touch of a button**.
5) **Electronic fund transfer** is used to pay suppliers and accept payment from customers. Electronic Fund Transfer at Point Of Sale (**EFTPOS**) systems such as Maestro and Delta allow customers to pay for goods direct from their bank account.
6) Computers are also used in **credit control**. Letters are printed out **automatically** to send to customers who are behind on payments.

EPOS and EFTPOS aren't the same thing. EPOS is explained on p.62

IT has had an impact on **Location** and **Employment**

1) More workers are able to **work from home** using email to communicate with the office. This is called **teleworking**.
2) The benefit of teleworking to the **employee** is that teleworkers can work more **flexible hours**, while still being able to communicate with their colleagues.
3) The benefit to the **employer** is that the employer doesn't have to **pay** for teleworkers' heating, lighting or health and safety.
4) Many businesses are now able to locate in **cheaper areas** because they can **use technology** to **communicate** with **customers**, e.g. call centre staff can bring up a customer's whole history on the computer screen, rather than looking through paper files, or dealing with the customer face-to-face.
5) Online businesses and call centres are free to locate **anywhere in the world** where labour is cheap. During the late 90s and early 00s, many call centres relocated to India.

Investing in IT can be **Costly**

1) New IT equipment or software can be **expensive** to buy. Also, staff will need to be **trained** to use it — the training will cost money and production **time** is **lost** whilst the training is carried out.
2) If there are **problems** with IT, e.g. **equipment breaking** or **systems crashing**, it can halt production or mean communications are hampered. It will also take time to investigate and fix the problem.

Practice Questions

Q1 Why do most large retailers now use EPOS systems?

Q2 State one reason why a business might use CAD when designing a new product.

Q3 What is a teleworker, and why might workers be more motivated if they are given the opportunity to become a teleworker?

Exam Questions

Q1 Evaluate the effect of the internet upon a typical high street clothing retailer. (12 marks)

Q2 "The introduction of an Electronic Point of Sale (EPOS) system will mean that never again will customers be faced with an empty shelf". Discuss the extent to which you agree with this statement. (12 marks)

I still say "bring on the robots"...

I wonder how operations control was handled before there were computers — there must have been an awful lot of paper flying around the office. You're expected to know about various uses of IT in stock control, production, communication, finance and location. There are probably more than you'd think, so learn these pages carefully.

Location

A fundamental decision for any business organisation is where to locate its factory, distribution centre or admin HQ. Lots of factors come into consideration.

Location Decisions are based on Quantitative Cost-Benefit Analysis

1) When deciding where to locate, businesses analyse the potential impact on **costs** and **revenues**. Businesses use **quantitative analysis** techniques such as **break-even analysis** and **investment appraisal analysis** to assess this.
2) Businesses calculate how many sales they'll need to break even at each location. Where the **costs of operating** from a location are **high** (e.g. because of high labour costs or high ground rents), the **break even output** will be higher. It's preferable to locate where break-even output is low. See p.30-31 for more on break-even.
3) Location or relocation of a business is a big **investment**. Businesses do **investment appraisal analysis** to calculate the **payback period**, **accounting rate of return** and **internal rate of return**. See p.34-37 for more on this.

Quantitative Factors affect choice of Location

Location decisions depend on distribution and supply costs

1) **Manufacturing** businesses which provide **bulky finished products** should be located near to their **customers** to cut down on distribution costs. Bulky products made from **lightweight** components are called "**bulk increasing**" commodities.
2) Other products need **bulky raw materials** to make a **lightweight end product** — these are "**bulk decreasing**" commodities. They need to be located near the source of **raw materials** to keep transport costs down.
3) A good **transport infrastructure** cuts distribution costs.
4) **Services** don't have large distribution costs. Decisions on where to locate services are based mainly on other criteria.

E.g. beer — made of water (available anywhere), plus hops and barley (low in bulk compared to the finished product). Breweries tend to be located near consumers and transport infrastructure, not near hop or barley fields.

E.g. the steel industry in South Wales. The three basic ingredients are iron ore (imported to local ports), coal and limestone (both from South Wales). The product is rolled steel, which is less bulky and can be transported by rail.

Location decisions depend on the availability and cost of resources

1) There must be a **good supply** of labour resources in the area where a business will be located.
2) The labour force must also be **suitable** — e.g. they might need to be literate, they might need special skills such as IT, technical knowledge of machinery, etc.
3) The area might need **local training facilities** for staff e.g. a college or university.
4) The area needs **facilities** such as affordable housing, suitable schooling, medical facilities, retail and leisure outlets to provide a good **quality of living** for staff.
5) Businesses can afford to pay workers less in areas where the **cost of living** is lower. To take full advantage of this, businesses need to locate overseas where labour costs are far lower than in the UK — see p.66.
6) Businesses also need the right land resources. There may be a requirement for room for **future expansion**.
7) The **cost** of **land** and **property** for factories and business premises varies significantly from area to area — land in the London area is far more expensive than land in mid Wales, for example.
8) **International** location decisions must take account of variations in the cost of water and **electricity**.

Location decisions depend on the market

1) Some businesses such as **retailers** need to locate **near to customers**, in order to catch the passing trade.
2) Businesses prefer to be based in locations which will **maximise their revenue**.

A good location needs an efficient and appropriate infrastructure

1) Business organisations benefit from access to **motorways**, fast **rail** links, **sea ports** and **airports**.
2) Transport infrastructure is needed for the **import** of **raw materials**, the **distribution** of **finished products**, and for **staff** to get to work.
3) Businesses also need **support services**. Most business organisations need some form of **commercial** support such as **banking**, **insurance** and **marketing** agencies.
4) Often there's a need for **technical** support such as engineering services and **IT** assistance.

Location

Some Locations benefit from Government Incentives

Successive governments have attempted to attract business organisations to areas with high **unemployment**.

They use both "**carrots**" and "**sticks**" to encourage businesses to locate in deprived areas. An example of a "**carrot**" would be a **grant** given to a business locating in an area of high unemployment. An example of a **"stick"** would be **refusing planning permission** to build a factory in an area where there are already lots of jobs.

1) Since the 1970s, the UK government has set up **Development Agencies** for Scotland, Wales, Northern Ireland and the English regions, to coordinate and encourage development. These development agencies get money from **central government** to spend on attracting businesses to their area.
2) They can provide **financial assistance** to business through grants, loans and equity (share) investment. They also provide **financial guidance** and **management support**.
3) They can also help businesses find the right sort of **property** to locate in.

1) The UK government has also set up **Enterprise Zones** to attract new business. They offer **tax breaks**, and reduce the amount of paperwork that businesses have to complete. Enterprise zones last for 10 years.
2) Within Enterprise Zones, there's financial assistance with **property** — businesses don't have to pay the full rate of tax for capital expenditure on buildings, and they don't have to pay the full **rates** (tax on business premises).
3) **Planning rules** and other regulations are made **simpler**, and **government paperwork** is processed more **quickly**.

There are also Qualitative Factors involved in Choosing a Location

1) Entrepreneurs might choose to start a business near where they **live** — e.g. Dyson is based in Wiltshire, near the owner and inventor's home.
2) Some places have a **good image** which suits the image of the product. High fashion works better in New York, London and Paris than in Scunthorpe or Workington — New York, London and Paris already have a fashion image.

All these factors rarely, if ever, combine in one place to create an **ideal** location. It's more likely that the decision of where to locate a business is based on a **compromise** between different factors.

Businesses may have to Relocate — move facilities somewhere else

1) Established businesses sometimes have to up sticks and **move**. This may be because the firm has **grown too large** for its premises, or because **government incentives** have been withdrawn, or because taxes have risen.
2) Some organisations have "**industrial inertia**". This is where they choose to set up in a location because of particular factors, but then these original factors become unimportant or disappear and the firm doesn't move.
3) Deciding where to relocate is similar to deciding where to locate, with some added problems:
   - Production is likely to be reduced during the move — there may be **downtime**.
   - **Staff** may not **want** to move. They may need to be **paid** to relocate, especially if they have dependent family.
   - Notifying **suppliers** and **customers** costs money. Updating **headed notepaper** and **brochures** costs money.

Practice Questions

Q1 Identify and briefly explain three factors which affect location cost.

Q2 What are Enterprise Zones?

Q3 What factors can cause problems for a firm wishing to relocate?

Exam Question

Q1 What factors should a firm that produces plastic bottles consider when deciding where to locate a new factory? (10 marks)

Phil and Kirsty can't help you now...

You're going to have to learn the factors which affect business location, no "maybe"s about it. If this comes up in the exam (more than likely) you'll probably get a case study with some facts and figures about a business, and you'll be asked to say why the business chose to locate where it did. Or you might have to write a report recommending a location for a business.

Locating Abroad

Businesses may decide to locate production abroad.

Multinationals *are located in* ***Several Countries***

Multinational corporations (**MNC**s for short) are large manufacturing and trading organisations with their **headquarters** in one country and bases in other countries. MNCs tend to locate their **headquarters** in a more economically developed country (**MEDC**) and their **manufacturing** plants in less economically developed countries (**LEDCs**).

Locating ***Abroad*** *can* ***Reduce Costs*** *— and incur some new costs*

Advantages of locating abroad

1) MNCs locate production facilities in countries with **low labour costs**. LEDCs such as Bangladesh, Vietnam and Malaysia have a large supply of low cost unskilled and semi-skilled labour. Many manufacturers of electrical goods, clothing etc. have located production facilities in these countries.
2) The cost of **land** and **buildings** is also significantly lower in LEDCs.
3) LEDCs tend to have much **looser employment laws** than the UK — e.g. there's often no minimum holiday requirement and far fewer health and safety regulations. This reduces the cost of **production**.
4) Often, host countries have **lower tax** rates. A lower tax bill is appealing to any business.
5) Locating in several countries **weakens trade union** power — a business with factories in just **one country** is vulnerable to **trade union action**. A business with factories in **several countries** won't have to stop production altogether if a union in one country goes on strike.

Disadvantages of locating abroad

1) Of course, relocating abroad **incurs costs** of its own. **Equipment** may have to be moved abroad — which is very **expensive**. It's best if equipment can be **sourced locally**.
2) Moving UK production abroad means making all your UK production workers **redundant**, which costs money.
3) Businesses can end up chasing low labour costs from one country to another. For example, Nike had shoe factories in **South Korea** in the late 1980s. They moved a lot of these to **China** and **Indonesia** in the mid 1990s, and they're now getting their shoes assembled in **Vietnam**.
4) Executives have to **travel** abroad between all the different sites, but this cost is relatively **low** and can be reduced by use of ICT such as email, telephone conferencing and videoconferencing.
5) **Exchange rates** affect the cost of business. By producing in the same market where goods are sold, businesses get around the problem of exchange rates going up and down.

It's better from this point of view to make goods for the UK market in the UK, goods for the US market in the US, goods for Japan in Japan, etc.

Case Study — Dyson in Malaysia

Background: The vacuum cleaner and washing machine manufacturer Dyson was originally set up in the UK. Their HQ and manufacturing facilities were both located in Malmesbury, in Wiltshire, southern England.

Relocation: Production of vacuum cleaners was moved to Malaysia in 2002, with the loss of 800 jobs in Malmesbury, Wiltshire. Production of washing machines went to Malaysia in 2003, with the loss of 65 more jobs.

Benefits of location in Malaysia: Production costs would be 30% lower in Malaysia than the UK. At the time of the relocation, Malaysian workers were paid one third of the wages of UK workers. At the time of the relocation, office space in Malaysia cost one third of the rental cost of office space in the UK.

Disadvantages of location in the UK: Apart from the high cost of production in the UK, the local government had refused planning permission for enlargement of the vacuum cleaner production factory in Malmesbury.

Jobs in UK: Research and development and head office jobs remained in Malmesbury. The company's owner, James Dyson, claimed that moving production to Malaysia enabled the company to enlarge R&D facilities in Malmesbury, creating more skilled jobs in Wiltshire.

Locating Abroad *can help businesses to* ***Grow***

1) MNCs can take advantage of **new markets** in the host country. This is particularly beneficial when the home market is **saturated**.
2) By operating on a **worldwide scale**, firms can grow **very large**, and gain the benefits of **economies of scale**.

Locating Abroad

Host Countries offer *Incentives* to tempt businesses to locate there

Governments of host countries are keen for foreign companies to locate facilities there. Multinationals bring **jobs**, which boosts the host nation's economy.

Governments of host countries are often willing to **pay incentives** to foreign companies — sometimes over 50% of the cost of a production facility. They see it as **investment** in the economy.

Locating Abroad can get around *Trade Barriers*

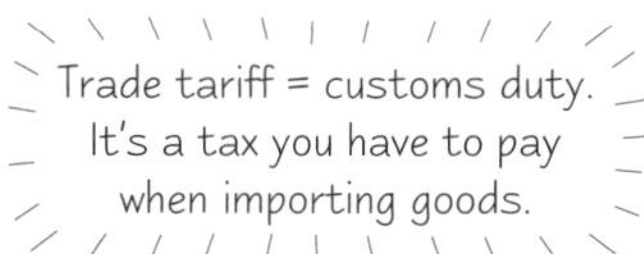

1) MNCs who want to trade in foreign countries with **high trade tariffs** need to **locate there** to get round the tariffs. **China** has barriers to trade which mean it's difficult and expensive to export to China unless you have a base in China.
2) The **European Union** is a common trading market. There are no trade tariffs on trade **between** EU member states, but companies based outside the EU have to pay a tariff on imports into the EU. It makes sense for companies **based outside** the EU to set up facilities **within** the EU. This allows them to sell to EU countries **without** paying a tariff, which makes their goods much more competitive.

Case Study — Toyota and Nissan car plants in the UK

Background: **Japanese** car manufacturers **Toyota** and **Nissan** both wanted a foothold in Europe to get around **EU trade barriers**.

Why the UK: The UK has less red tape than the rest of Europe. It's easier to dismiss workers, for example. The UK government offered **incentives**. Nissan and Toyota had **strong market share** in the UK.

Toyota: Toyota located a factory in Derbyshire in 1989, production started in 1992. The site had space to expand, a supply of skilled **workers**, and good **road** and **rail** links for bringing in parts and distributing finished cars.

Nissan: In 1984 Nissan located a factory in **Sunderland**. Production started in 1986. Sunderland had a supply of skilled workers, and good **road** and **rail** links, plus a nearby port.

Multinational involvement has *Pros* and *Cons* for *Customers* and *Workers*

	Advantages of multinational involvement	Disadvantages of multinational involvement
Workers	MNCs provide **employment**. Workers learn new **skills**.	**Working conditions** may be **poor**, with long hours and low health and safety standards. MNCs introduce their own managers, so little opportunity for **promotion**.
Consumers	MNCs offer **cheap prices** for UK consumer. **Host country** consumers have more money.	Goods may be of **lower quality**. Goods produced may not meet **host country needs**.
Host state	**Employment** and **national wealth** increase. MNCs bring **technology** and **investment**.	Most profit goes **overseas**. MNCs often **outcompete** local business.

Practice Questions

Q1 What is a multinational?

Q2 Give three examples of costs that can be reduced by locating abroad.

Q3 Why might a host government offer to pay incentives to a multinational?

Exam Questions

Q1 Catterick Cookwares are considering relocating production to Eastern Europe. Examine the factors they would take into account when making this decision. (10 marks)

Q2 Describe the advantages and disadvantages of a multinational manufacturing business setting up in an LEDC to the potential employees and to the host government. (8 marks)

If only I could relocate to the Bahamas — that'd suit me...

When deciding where to locate internationally a business has to consider all the factors that normally affect location decisions. This includes the infrastructure of the country, resources and workforce available, the local markets, costs involved and potential language problems. Then there's government incentives, economies of scale, the list just goes on...

Economic Variables

Interest rates, exchange rates, inflation and unemployment all affect business strategy.

Interest is the Price Paid for Borrowing Money

1) Interest rates show the **cost of borrowing**. The interest rate is set by the Bank of England.
2) A **fall** in the interest rate makes businesses **increase** their level of activity, because it's **cheaper** for them to borrow money to invest in the business.
3) A **rise** in the interest rate makes businesses **decrease** their activity, because it's **more expensive** for them to borrow money to invest.
4) Interest rates also affect **consumer spending**. High interest rates mean **less disposable income**. People with existing **borrowing** like **mortgages** have to pay more money back in **interest**, and consumers **save more money** because they get a better rate of return on it. When people have less disposable income, market **demand** goes down.
5) The effect that interest rates have on demand depends on the **product**. Products that require **borrowing** (e.g. cars, houses, new kitchens and high-end consumer electronics) are more sensitive to interest rate changes. When interest rates go up significantly, businesses change strategy to diversify away from these products and into cheaper goods.
6) Businesses compare UK interest rates to interest rates **abroad**. When the UK interest rate is higher, or more volatile than abroad, businesses are likely to invest in **foreign countries** with low, stable interest rates, as it's **cheaper** to borrow money to invest in expansion.
7) Remember **Internal Rate of Return** from p.36 — it's an investment appraisal technique that works out the required rate of return from a project so that it beats investing money in the bank. Clearly, the higher the interest rate, the better the project must be predicted to do before the business will go ahead with it. Again, high interest rates mean **less investment**, fewer **new projects** and less **expansion**.

Exchange Rate is the Value of One Currency in terms of Another Currency

1) Exchange rates affect the amount of **foreign trade**.

- When the exchange rate is **high** (e.g. more euros to the pound, £1 = 3 euros), UK **exports** are relatively **expensive** in Europe and **imports** into the UK are relatively **cheap** for Brits. A **strong pound** is **bad** for UK exporters because their goods aren't competitively priced abroad.
- When the exchange rate is **low** (e.g. less euros to the pound, £1 = 1 euro), UK **exports** are relatively **cheap** for foreigners and **imports** into the UK are relatively **expensive** for Brits.

2) A **strong pound** and **cheaper imports** mean **lower costs** for UK businesses importing raw materials from abroad, but they're bad news for UK manufacturers who export goods abroad.
3) When a rise in the value of the pound is predicted, a business might decide to move its **production** abroad. The business can also consider **importing** the **raw material** from abroad.
4) **Cheaper exports** should lead to increased **demand** and therefore higher **output**.

Exchange Rate Fluctuations create Uncertainty

1) E.g. a UK manufacturer agrees a contract to sell to the USA, and agrees to be paid in **US dollars**. At this point £1 = $1.50 and the contract is for $150,000 (£100,000). After the deal is made, the pound rises in value against the dollar, £1 is now worth $2. The dollar payment in the contract is now worth **fewer pounds** than before, so the UK manufacturer makes **less profit** from the contract than predicted, ($150,000 ÷ 2 = £75,000).
2) Let's say that the UK manufacturer insists on being paid in **pounds**. When the pound rises in value, the goods are more expensive in dollar terms for the US firm. They put the **selling price** up to compensate. The increase in price reduces **demand** for the goods, and there may be **less revenue** than predicted.

Some manufacturers based in the UK and **exporting to the EU** are considering **relocating** to **Euro zone** countries, so that their costs are in euros — the same currency their customers pay in. They may also decide to pay UK suppliers in euros, again to keep costs in the same currency that their customers pay them. See p.74 for more on the euro.

Economic Variables

Inflation affects *Consumer Spending* and *Business Strategy*

Inflation is an **increase** in the **price** of **goods** and **services**. The main measure of inflation in the UK is the **Retail Price Index** (RPI) — it lists the prices of hundreds of goods and services that the average household would buy.
It's the duty of the **Bank of England** to keep the inflation rate within a target range set by the Government.

1) When inflation is high, **spending goes up temporarily** — people **rush to buy more** before prices go up even more. If wages don't go up in line with inflation, spending goes down as people can afford less.
2) It's easier to **plan** when inflation is low. Stable prices mean businesses can make **accurate sales forecasts**.
3) Inflation caused by rising costs makes **profit margins** go **down** if businesses decide not to put up their prices.
4) Inflation caused by **excess demand** (demand-pull inflation) can make **profit margins** go **up**. Businesses operating at or near full capacity can put up prices in response to **high demand** without their **costs** going up by as much. Businesses may decide to **expand** during demand-pull inflation, to take advantage of increased demand.
5) When inflation in the UK is high, it makes UK **exports** expensive abroad. UK businesses become **less competitive**. When inflation in the UK is low, UK businesses have a competitive advantage.

Unemployment is measured by the number of *People Seeking Work*

1) Unemployment is measured by the number of jobless people who are a) **available** for work, and b) **actively seeking jobs**.
2) High unemployment can affect **sales**. Producers of **luxury** goods are badly affected by **cyclical** unemployment (caused by a downturn in the business cycle). Businesses producing **essentials** aren't affected much.
3) **Structural** unemployment is due to changes in the structure of the economy, e.g. a **decline** in a **major industry** such as coal mining. It's often concentrated in particular regions of the country. **Structural** unemployment affects **local** businesses — unemployed people in the area have little money to spend.
4) When unemployment is **high**, businesses can hire staff easily. There's a good **supply** of labour, so businesses won't have to pay **high wages**. People in work will be extra **productive** to protect their job.
5) If unemployment is **structural** or **regional**, it's not all that easy to hire staff. Unemployed workers often aren't in the **right place** or the **right industry** for the jobs that are out there. Unemployed workers from an industry in decline need **training** before they can do jobs in other industries.

The *Different Economic Variables* are all *Linked*

1) **Higher interest rates** attract capital from **overseas investors**, who want good return on their investment.
2) This inflow of money increases the **demand for sterling**, and causes the **exchange rate** to **rise**. The exchange rate is the **price of pounds sterling** in terms of another currency, remember. When the demand for something rises, the price rises as well — that's how markets work.
3) As the exchange rate rises, **imports** become **cheaper**. Prices drop — in other words the **inflation rate falls**.

Practice Questions

Q1 What is inflation?

Q2 How does a rise in interest rate affect: a) business activity, and b) consumer spending?

Q3 What is structural unemployment?

Exam Questions

Q1 Explain why high UK interest rates cause problems for a business producing expensive audio equipment. (14 marks)

Q2 Discuss the strategies that a manufacturing business can employ to respond to a rise in the value of the pound compared to the US dollar and the euro. (16 marks)

Your interest in this may well be flagging by now...

Make sure you understand how the different economic variables can have a big impact on businesses. Inflation can cause revenue to increase, but the price of raw materials and the cost of wages could also increase. Changes in interest rates affect the interest payments on loans and customer spending. Exchange rates affect international competitiveness.

The Business Cycle

The business cycle is the regular pattern of ups and downs in the economy. It affects business strategy.

The Business Cycle is a regular pattern of Growth and Recession

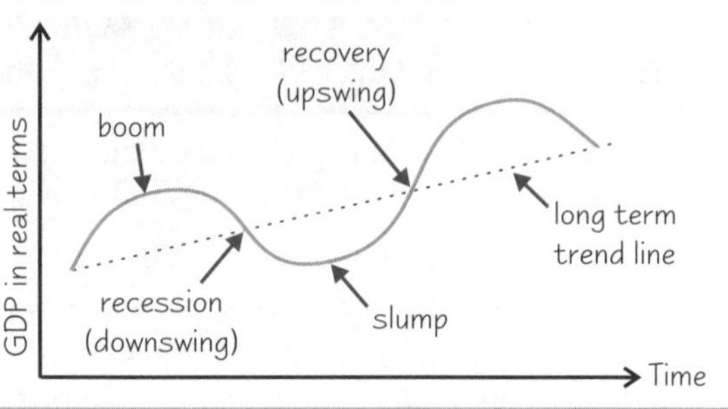

1) In a **recovery** or upswing, **production increases**, and **employment** increases. People have more money to spend.
2) In a **boom**, production levels are high. As production reaches **maximum capacity**, there are **shortages**, and price increases. Shortages of skilled labour mean **wages rise**.
3) In a **recession** incomes start to go down, and **demand** goes down. Business **confidence** is reduced.
4) In a **slump**, production is at a **low**. Businesses close factories and there are a lot of **redundancies**. **Unemployment** is **high**. A lot of businesses become **insolvent** or **bankrupt**.
5) The extent to which a business is **affected** by the business cycle depends on the **income elasticity of demand** of its products. Businesses selling **income elastic** goods such as luxury holidays find that demand shoots **up** in a **recovery**, and dives **down** in a **recession**. Businesses selling **income inelastic** goods such as staple foods **aren't affected** all that much by the business cycle.

Income elasticity of demand = extent that demand depends on customer income.

Businesses change their Strategy to deal with the Business Cycle

Upswing	1) During an **upswing** businesses can increase production. They may come out with **new products** to take advantage of increased **consumer income**. 2) They can invest in **fixed assets**, including machinery to replace labour. 3) They can increase their **capacity utilisation** to near optimal levels.
Boom	1) During **booms** businesses can **raise prices**. This increases profitability, and it slows down demand a bit. Businesses may have to increase prices to cover their own costs if there are wage rises due to shortages of labour. 2) In a long lasting boom, businesses **invest** in **production** facilities to increase capacity. They may increase output by producing overseas. 3) Because a **recession** is on the way, managers should **prepare for falling demand**.
Recession	1) During **recessions** businesses can make workers **redundant** or put them on a shorter working week. This **saves wage costs**. 2) During a local recession, they may also **subcontract** their production facilities to other businesses in order to increase capacity utilisation. 3) In a recession, businesses emphasise **value for money** and **competitive prices** in their advertising. This is to **increase demand** from customers with low incomes. 4) During a **local recession**, businesses can **market** their goods elsewhere in the country, e.g. a local shop could go mail-order. In a **national recession**, businesses can **market** their products **overseas** to increase sales.
Slump	1) During a slump businesses need to keep very **tight credit control**. 2) **Wages** have to be cut. 3) Businesses may diversify into basic, **income inelastic goods** and sell no-frills products at **bargain prices**. 4) When the national recession or slump lasts a long time, businesses may have to **relocate** abroad.

Governments try to make the Business Cycle go Slowly and Gently

1) In a **recession**, governments **cut taxes** (see p.76) to make businesses more **confident**, and to give people more **money** to spend. They can also increase **government spending** on benefits, and on building roads and schools.
2) In a **boom**, the government needs to control inflation by reducing demand. They reduce people's spending power by **raising taxes** and **cutting spending**.

These are called countercyclical policies.

The Labour Market

The Labour Market is a key external influence

Labour is obviously a very important **resource** needed for the production of output. Labour **costs** the business money in the form of **wages**.

The **demand** for labour is the firm's **willingness to employ labour** (at a particular wage).

1) An increase in wages will increase the **cost of production**. This in turn will raise the **prices** of products, which will reduce the **demand** for those goods. As demand for goods falls, demand for labour will decrease.
2) Also, the demand for labour will **fall** when labour can be substituted by a **cheaper alternative**, i.e. capital expenditure on machinery.

Chipmunks won't work for less than two peanuts per hour these days.

The **supply** of labour is the employees' **willingness to work** (at a particular wage).

1) As wages rise, the **supply** of labour **rises** — higher wages **attract workers** from other industries and those who are currently unemployed.
2) As wages **fall**, the supply of labour goes down, because people aren't willing to work for peanuts.

Low Unemployment is linked to Skills Shortages

1) As well as a labour surplus or shortage, you can also have a **skills surplus** or **shortage**. Skills surpluses are (fairly obviously) where you have more people with a particular skill (e.g. steelworking) than jobs which use that skill. This means that businesses can pay less for these workers as there are more workers than jobs. Skills shortages are where you don't have enough workers with the right skills to fill available skilled jobs.
2) There are **shortages** of skilled labour in many industries.
3) Skills shortages are solved by **training**, but training is **expensive**. Governments can help by providing **training schemes** and pushing colleges to offer **vocational** (job-related) courses and qualifications. Businesses who invest in training can find that competitors **poach** employees once they're trained.
4) Businesses can get round skills shortages by investing in labour saving **machinery** — in other words, switching from labour intensive production to **capital intensive** production.
5) Businesses can also get round skills shortages by **relocating production** or service provision **abroad** where there are plenty of skilled workers — e.g. to India.
6) They may also **import workers** from overseas. Workers from outside the EU need **work permits** to work in the UK. To get a work permit, their employer must show that they **can't get** a **UK** or **EU** person to fill the job vacancy.

Skills shortages are bad news for most businesses, but good news for recruitment consultants.

Capital intensive = tends to use machinery rather than human labour. Remember, machinery is a capital asset.

Practice Questions

Q1 Give an example of a way that a business might adapt their strategy to cope with a recession.

Q2 When should a business start to prepare for a recession?

Q3 What is the effect of a wage cut on the supply of labour?

Q4 How might a business respond to a skills shortage?

Exam Questions

Q1 Describe how a electronic goods retailer might successfully weather a slump. (14 marks)

Q2 Evaluate methods of coping with a skills shortage. (18 marks)

It'd sound more fun if they called it the "business rollercoaster"...

The basics of this are covered in AS level, so some of this isn't brand new to your eyes. Learn it all anyway, because you've probably forgotten half of it. Learn the whys and wherefores of the business cycle, and learn a couple of things that businesses do to cope with the cycle. As if that weren't enough, businesses have the labour market to deal with too.

Economic Growth

Economic growth affects both businesses and governments.

Economic Growth is the Increase in Size of a nation's Economy

1) Economic growth is an **increase** in the nation's production of **goods** and **services**.
2) It's measured as the **rate of increase in GDP** (Gross Domestic Product). **GDP** is the **total market value** of **goods** and **services** produced **by** a nation **within** that nation during a period of time. GDP is calculated in **real terms**, i.e. by ignoring **inflation**.

   GDP = total **consumer spending** + business **investment** + **government spending** + the value of **exports** – the value of **imports**.

3) Economic growth means the same thing as "an increase in **economic activity**" — growth means there's **more demand** in the economy and **more output** to meet that demand.

The rate of growth for the UK is estimated to be 2.5% per year.

Economic Growth is determined by Resources and Productivity

1) The **growth potential** of an economy depends on the **amount** and **quality** of economic **resources** available — e.g. labour and fixed assets.

Quantity and quality of labour	**Quantity** of labour depends on **population size**, and on its **age** composition. **Quality** of labour means the **education and training** that workers have. **High quality** of labour enables an economy to **grow faster**.
Investment	**Investment** increases the amount of **productive assets** (machinery etc. used for production). For **growth** to happen, the **level of investment** in productive assets has to be greater than the amount of **depreciation** (the amount by which machines wear out) during the year.

2) It also depends on their **productivity** — how hard the nation works.
3) **Governments** can encourage **short term** growth by cutting taxes and interest rates (see p.68 and p.76). This encourages businesses to borrow money and invest it in production. It also encourages consumers to borrow money and spend it on goods, which increases demand in the economy.
4) These days, economists tend to think it's better to **encourage steady growth** using "supply-side policies" which encourage **investment**, training and **employment**. These increase the **quality of labour**.

Economic Growth has Mainly Positive Effects for business and government

Economic **growth** means an increase in **national income**, which is usually good news.

Individual Businesses

1) **Growth** in GDP means **higher revenues** and higher **profitability** for **businesses**.
2) Economic growth gives the potential for **economies of scale**.
3) Sustained growth increases **confidence** and helps businesses **plan** for the future.
4) Fast growth may cause **shortages** of raw materials and skilled labour.
5) Fast growth causes inflation.

Governments

1) **Higher revenue** encourages investment in new projects, which creates jobs. This is good for the government — there's less need to pay welfare benefits.
2) Growth also enables the government to earn **increased revenues** through **taxes**.
3) Very high rates of growth are usually followed by **recession**. Governments try to avoid this boom-and-bust situation by keeping growth at a **sustainable** level.

It appears someone's gone a bit wild with the fertiliser.

The **Environment**

1) High levels of economic activity may deplete **non-renewable resources**.
2) Increased economic activity may also cause increased **pollution**.

There can be differences between Local, National and Global economic activity

Growth doesn't happen uniformly across the whole world, or even across a country. For example in the UK, the South East grew more than other regions in the 1990s. This uneven growth can be because of differences in **infrastructure**, **supply** of **workers**, **government incentives**, or whether a business needs to be close to its markets or suppliers.

International Competitiveness

Foreign Markets present *Opportunities* and *Threats*

1) Selling to a much **larger market** is a huge opportunity to **increase sales revenue** and grow your business. The world's your oyster, as the saying goes.
2) Selling to a larger market allows businesses to have **economies of scale**.
3) A business that has access to **many markets** has a lower risk of bankruptcy. Not all markets go down at the same time. In fact, a business may see **growth** in one market, and **recession** in another market at the same time. This helps the business **weather** the ups and downs of the business cycle.
4) Trading in international markets also presents a **threat**. Foreign businesses may be able to **undercut** domestic businesses on the domestic market and abroad.

Businesses *Trading Abroad* need to be *Internationally Competitive*

International competitiveness means the ability to **compete** with businesses **abroad**. To be internationally competitive, businesses need to integrate various factors to make themselves efficient, and in order to provide quality products that people across the world want to buy.

Price and quality

1) Businesses need to be competitive in terms of **price**. They need **efficient production** systems to keep **costs** and prices down. The most competitive businesses use lean production and the most efficient technology.
2) They also need to compete in terms of **quality**. High quality products can sell at a premium price. Sony, Philips, Porsche and BMW are examples of international businesses who compete successfully with low-cost rivals.

Employees

1) The workforce has to be **productive**.
2) This means they need to be **highly motivated**, and very **well trained**.

Marketing

1) Businesses trading abroad must **market** their products and services effectively to compete with foreign rivals. Huge global businesses such as **Coca Cola** and **General Motors** market their goods very successfully, and they are particularly good at getting into **new markets** all over the world.
2) Good **public image** and **customer goodwill** is a part of marketing. For example, the international oil giant BP tries to project an **environmentally friendly image** by publicising its research into sustainable energy.
3) Some multinational businesses **localise** their **marketing**. They market their products differently in **different countries**.

Government Policy

Governments have a role in international competitiveness, because they can create an economic environment that's **favourable** to businesses.

1) A **stable economy** and a **well educated workforce** make it easier for businesses to be competitive right across the world.
2) **Exchange rates** affect international competitiveness — see p.68.

Practice Questions

Q1 Give two examples of factors which encourage economic growth.

Q2 What are the effects of economic growth on governments?

Q3 Give an example of a strategy to maintain international competitiveness.

Exam Questions

Q1 Discuss the negative effects of rapid economic growth for a small manufacturer of office supplies. (14 marks)

Q2 "Productive efficiency is the key determinant of economic growth." Evaluate this statement. (16 marks)

If you didn't get growth in the garden centre market, you'd be worrying...

Growth in the national economy is a good thing for business, and for society in general. The problems come when growth is too fast — production can't keep up, and a pleasant period of growth swings round into an unpleasant recession. Remember that this is a problem for governments as well as businesses.

The European Union

The EU is a union of 25 independent countries, with a population of over 450 million — bigger than the US and Japan put together. Ten new countries joined in 2004, and more have applied to join. It's a big deal.

*The EU is a **Single Market** — **Trade** between member states is **Easy***

1) There aren't **trade barriers** between EU member states — this is called the Single Market. Businesses don't pay **tax** when they **import** goods from other EU countries. The EU provides easy export opportunities for UK firms.
2) The EU has **customs union**, which means the **same customs duties** apply to all goods entering the area irrespective of which country they come from, and which country they're going to.
3) The Single Market **smooths out price differences** between member states. **Producers** can look for the **highest selling price** within the EU, and consumers can look for the **lowest purchase price** within the EU. When the price in part of the EU is high, producers flood that area with their product, driving down prices. Low prices attract more buyers to the market, pushing prices up.
4) There's freedom of movement of all "factors of production" within the EU. That covers **raw materials**, **finished goods** and **workers**. EU citizens can work in any country of the EU.
5) A common **EU competition law** controls anti-competitive activities — e.g. setting up a **monopoly**.
6) There are **common policies** on **product regulation** as well.

*The **Growth** of the **EU** has increased **Business Opportunities***

1) Whenever the EU expands, the **size of the market** available to an EU based producer increases. Businesses can enjoy **increased sales** and take advantage of **economies of scale.**
2) The EU collectively has **more political whack** than its member states. For example, the EU can negotiate any trade dispute with the USA on equal terms. This increases competitiveness.
3) **Production costs** are **low** in the **new EU countries** that joined in 2004 such as Poland, Hungary and Slovakia. Businesses can locate production facilities there to increase their competitiveness.

Increased Competition** in the EU can be a **Threat

1) The expansion of the EU also brings **businesses** from **new member states** into the market.
2) There's **increased competition** in industries where new member states such as Hungary and Poland have an advantage — e.g. **manufacturing** and **agriculture**. This threatens UK manufacturers and farmers. Polish farmers can produce food more **cheaply**.
3) Increased competition may also hurt **inefficient** producers in the new member states, who were previously serving protected national markets.
4) But **high tech** UK businesses can keep their **competitive advantage**.

*The **Euro** is the **Common Currency** of **Most EU Countries***

1) The euro became the **common currency** of 11 EU member states in **1999**. They completely changed over from their old currencies in **2002**. These countries are commonly called the **euro zone**. Changing to the euro was the final stage in the plan for **European Monetary Union** (EMU).
2) All these euro zone countries have the **same interest rate**, and the **same exchange rate** with **other currencies**. This means euro zone businesses can sell stuff to each other without the **hassle** and **uncertainty** of constantly changing exchange rates.
3) **Changing money** on the foreign exchange market **costs money**. The common currency **reduces transaction costs** between businesses in different euro zone countries.
4) It's also easy to **check prices** between euro zone countries.
5) The **UK** isn't in the euro zone, so UK businesses exporting abroad face the **uncertainty** of fluctuating exchange rates. When the **pound rises in value** against the euro, UK exporters **lose** international competitiveness because their goods become more **expensive** for euro zone countries.
6) Many UK businesses trading in the euro zone **price** and **trade** in the euro to make things easier. UK **banks** offer **euro accounts**, but there's a charge for them, so they may not be **cost effective** for businesses who mainly trade in the UK.
7) Governments of euro zone countries **can't control** interest rates, inflation or exchange rates. This means they are unable to use these **economic variables** to control their country's economy and so they **can't** use them to **help improve** the competitiveness of their own country's businesses.

The European Union

*It's **Difficult** for businesses to come up with **Pan-European Strategy***

1) It's easy for businesses to think of EU as a big single market, with same rules and regulations throughout. In reality, it's tricky to come up with a **pan-European strategy** — one that works all over Europe.
2) There are still **cultural differences** between countries, and lots of **different languages**, so EU businesses need to market products in different ways to suit **different countries**.
3) Having to do lots of marketing campaigns for one product **reduces economies of scale**.
4) There are also still **legal** differences between EU countries.

EU Institutions** pass **Laws** which affect **Business

EU laws are divided into **four main categories**:

1) **Regulations** are **binding laws** that apply to **all** EU citizens as soon as they're passed.
2) **Directives** tell **member state** governments to **pass a law** that meets a specific objective — e.g. reducing working time to 48 hours per week, reducing pollution. It's up to member state governments how to word the law. Some member governments make **strict** laws in response to EU directives, while others are more slack.
3) **Decisions** are **binding laws** that apply to a **specific country** or a **specific business**.
4) **Recommendations** aren't really laws at all, because they're **not legally binding**.

Most EU laws are directives.

The European Commission and the Council of Ministers decide on policies and laws

1) The **European Commission** puts forward new laws. The EU Commission is **appointed**, not elected.
2) The Council of Ministers **decides** whether or not to bring in **new laws** suggested by the Commission. It's made up of **government ministers** from **each member state**.

There's one commissioner from each member state.

The European Parliament gives its opinion on new laws

1) The European Parliament is **directly elected**, so it gives some democratic legitimacy to European law.
2) However, it's the Council of Ministers who have the final decision on laws, not the European Parliament.

The European Central Bank (ECB) controls the euro

1) The **ECB** decides monetary policy (interest rate) in the euro zone.
2) Only the euro zone countries have a say in the running of the bank.

The European Court of Justice interprets EU law

1) The European Court of Justice makes sure that **EU law** is applied in line with the **Treaty of Rome** — the treaty that says how the EU must be run.
2) It also sorts out disputes between member states.
3) The decisions of the court take precedence over the laws of each member state.

Practice Questions

Q1 Give an example of a benefit to business of the EU Single Market.

Q2 Give one benefit to business if the UK adopted the euro.

Q3 What is an EU directive?

Exam Questions

Q1 Analyse the ways in which a Welsh toy manufacturer would be affected if the UK decided to adopt the euro. (14 marks)

Q2 "The bureaucrats in Brussels can't change the way I run my business."
Do you accept this statement? Justify your answer. (14 Marks)

450 million people — that's a lot, boss...

The EU is a big deal for businesses — as the Single Market grows, there's more opportunity for easy importing and exporting. The EU is also another source of laws and regulations that businesses have to follow. Whether you're generally pro-Europe or anti-Europe doesn't change the fact that you need to revise both these pages to be prepared for the exam.

Government Policy

Government policy alters economic variables to change the level of economic activity.

Monetary Policy controls the Interest Rate

Monetary policy means **tweaking** the **interest rate** in order to control **inflation** and **exchange rates**.
The main objectives of a country's monetary policy should be:

1) Controlling **inflation.**
2) Controlling the overall rate of **economic growth.**
3) Managing the level of **unemployment.**
4) Influencing **foreign exchange rates.**

Even though the Bank of England sets interest rates independently, the Bank of England Monetary Policy Committee should bear the government's fiscal policy in mind when it makes its decisions. The Treasury has a non-voting representative at MPC meetings, who keeps the MPC up to date on fiscal policy decisions.

Fiscal Policy changes Taxes and Spending to Heat or Cool the Economy

1) **Fiscal policy** does **two** things — it sets **tax rates**, and it sets the amount of **government spending**.
2) **Raising taxes** cools the economy down, and cutting taxes heats it up — **low rates of tax** give businesses more profit, and **encourage business activity**.
    - It's fairly easy to predict the effects of a change in **direct taxation**. Raising **income tax** reduces consumer spending, and reduces business output.
    - **Indirect taxation** is slightly harder to predict. Increases in **VAT** cut consumer spending, but also **raise inflation**.
3) **Government spending** on social services, health, education etc., also heats up the economy.
    - Changing government expenditure on **welfare benefits** has a **quick** impact on the economy, because poorer people who receive benefits will change their spending habits straight away.
    - Government spending on **infrastructure** such as roads has a **slower** effect on the economy.
4) **Fiscal policy** is really about the **balance** between tax and spending.
The Chancellor of the Exchequer decides what the balance is going to be in the yearly Budget.

Fiscal Policy	How it's done	The effect it has
Expansionary fiscal policy	Cutting taxes and/or Raising spending	Government **borrowing increases** (or government **surplus decreases**)
Contractionary fiscal policy	Raising taxes and/or Cutting spending	Government **borrowing decreases** (or government **surplus increases**)

5) In times of **high unemployment** and economic slowdown the government may **borrow** money to spend, to **increase demand** for goods and services. This is **expansionary** fiscal policy.
6) The government may spend **less** than its revenue when high demand has pushed production to its limits, and threatens to bring on excessive inflation. This is **contractionary** fiscal policy.

Intervention vs Laissez-Faire — whether governments Interfere in the economy

1) The idea of **laissez-faire** says **governments shouldn't interfere** in the economy. The idea of **interventionism** says they **should** get involved.

Laissez-faire is French for "leave alone".

2) Governments **intervene** by charging taxes, passing laws which affect business, providing public services, taking part in the economy as a consumer, and providing subsidies. Some governments intervene more than others.
3) Governments that take a **laissez-faire** approach **dismantle** existing regulations that **constrain** business, abolish wage controls and **reduce taxation rates**.
4) The argument for **laissez-faire** is that **intervention raises costs** and makes business less **efficient** and less **profitable**. Allowing businesses to cut wages makes them more **competitive**. Supporters of laissez-faire say that it encourages individuals to be **responsible** instead of relying on the state.
5) **Interventionists** say governments must step in to ensure **fair competition**. Also, a totally **free**, totally **profit driven** market does things which create **social** and **environmental** costs.
See p.81 for more on market failure.

Government Policy

Nationalisation is Government Ownership and Control of Businesses

1) **Nationalisation** means taking businesses into **government ownership**. Supporters of nationalisation say it protects loss-making businesses, reduces expenditure on competition, and produces the goods society needs.
2) However, nationalisation **almost always fails**, because it ends up with a **legally protected monopoly**. Lack of competition often makes for inefficiency and poor quality. Nationalised industries often don't make much profit.

Privatisation is when State Owned Business are sold to Private Investors

1) In the 1980s and 1990s lots of state owned companies were sold off into the private sector. Examples include **British Telecom**, **British Gas**, **British Steel**, the **water** companies and the **electricity** distribution companies.
2) The government sold off these businesses to private investors to improve their **efficiency**, and to make a **profit**.

Benefits of privatisation	Drawbacks of privatisation
Privatisation **promotes competition**, which **increases efficiency**, and offers **better quality** products at **lower prices**.	**Some** privatised companies have **raised prices** and **cut quality** to **exploit** consumers — especially if they're effectively a **monopoly**.
The **government** has made a big **profit** from privatisation. This has helped the government to **cut taxes** and **reduce its borrowing**, which in turn **encourages business activity**.	Privatised companies tend to have **lots of shareholders** — often **private citizens** holding just a few shares. Shareholders tend to look for **quick profit** at the expense of **long term strategy**.

This profit is one-off profit — the privatisation can't be repeated.

3) Some industries are **natural monopolies**, for example, you wouldn't have several sets of rail tracks from one city to another. When privatising a natural monopoly like the **railways**, the government needs to build in regulations to prevent the new owners from exploiting their position and raising prices or cutting quality.

Case study: Railtrack

Privatisation: The UK government privatised the railways, and placed them under control of Railtrack. Railtrack was effectively a monopoly, with train operating companies as its customers.

Regulation: The Government set up the Office of the Rail Regulator (ORR) to keep an eye on Railtrack. The ORR had to make sure that Railtrack did not allow its commercial interest to get in the way of public standards and safety.

Practice Questions

Q1 What are the two component parts of fiscal policy?

Q2 Explain two ways in which governments intervene in the economy.

Q3 Why do some privatised industries need to be regulated?

Exam Questions

Q1 Outline the effects a contractionary fiscal policy could have on a restaurant business. (14 marks)

Q2 Describe the arguments for and against government intervention in the economy. (16 marks)

Q3 "Privatisation must create competition." Discuss. (18 marks)

I thought we elected governments to think about all this for us...

All the stuff on these pages affects everyone in some way — tax rates affect everyone, and government spending affects everyone too. Political parties fight elections on this sort of thing. Of course, that doesn't mean that you wouldn't rather be doing something else than revising this. Sure, I sympathise. But I can't make it go away. You'll have to learn it some time...

Social and Environmental Influences

Society and environmental concerns affect business.

Social Responsibility *means being responsible towards the* ***Whole of Society***

1) Corporate social responsibility is the **voluntary** role of business in looking after **society** and the environment.
2) Businesses have special responsibility to their **stakeholders** — everyone who's affected by the business, e.g. **employees**, **suppliers**, **creditors**, **customers**, **shareholders** and local **communities**.

Employees

1) Every firm has **legal responsibilities** to its staff.
2) Firms have a responsibility to **train** employees.
3) Firms can **choose** to give their employees a better deal than the bare legal minimum. Firms that operate internationally can **choose** to give workers abroad similar rights to workers in the UK.

Examples — providing a safe work environment, not discriminating based on race or gender, giving lunch breaks and paid holiday. See p.50.

Suppliers

1) It's not in a firm's best interest to treat their **suppliers** badly. For good results, be **honest** and **pay** on time.
2) Firms can build **long-term relationships** with suppliers — e.g. by offering **long-term exclusive supply contracts** and placing **regular orders**. A good loyal relationship makes it more likely that the supplier will pull all the stops out to deliver **fast service** when it's really needed.
3) There's also a responsibility to the rest of **society** to choose suppliers who don't **exploit** their workers or **pollute** excessively. Firms may not see this as worthwhile, **unless** customers care enough to **boycott** the product.

Customers

1) Firms who treat their **customers** well can build up **customer goodwill**. Good customer service, good quality products and reasonable prices all encourage **customer loyalty** and **repeat business**.
2) Customers are more and more willing to **complain** when firms don't treat them well. Customers can even **campaign against** firms who disappoint, and **persuade** other people **not to buy** their goods and services.

Local Community

1) Firms can be responsible to the local community by keeping **jobs secure**, and using **local suppliers**.
2) They can also avoid **noise pollution**, **air pollution** and excess **traffic** on local roads.
3) Businesses can **earn goodwill** by making **charity** donations or **sponsoring** schools, leisure centres, parks etc.

Some people think that firms should only be responsible to their **shareholders** and no one else.

Business Ethics *help businesses make* ***Socially Responsible Decisions***

1) Ethics means a shared set of attitudes and morals. Business ethics is about doing the "**right thing**". Not everyone **agrees** on what's ethical and what's not. For example, most people agree that child labour is unethical, but opinions differ on whether it's unethical to sell cigarettes even though they cause cancer.
2) Until recently, business ethics was considered almost a contradiction in terms — why would businesses choose to be "**nice**". Of course, there's a benefit in being "**nice**" to **stakeholders**. Taking an ethical stance **attracts customers** who **approve** of the decision. An ethical approach can be a **unique selling point**, particularly in retail (e.g. Body Shop toiletries, Fairtrade coffee, etc). Ethics can be **good PR**.
3) The **corporate culture** (see p.88) of a business affects its ethics. For example, in an environment that is heavily oriented to meeting sales targets, sales staff may be tempted to act unethically to get more commission. It's up to management to set **ethical guidelines** to make sure staff don't act dishonestly.
4) When introducing a **new ethical policy**, senior management have to set out **firm guidelines**, and make ethical policy part of **training** for new and established employees. In a business environment with a high degree of **delegation**, it can be **difficult** for senior management to push through a new ethical policy. Junior managers and employees who are used to managing their own work may **resent** being told what to do.

- Businesses may be tempted to **exploit** their workers, particularly in countries with weak labour laws. Many businesses have a **policy** against "sweat-shop" labour or child labour. Examples are IKEA and Levi Strauss.
- Businesses may be tempted to **charge high prices** for important goods such as medicines. For example, drug companies agreed to lower prices of anti-HIV drugs in South Africa, but only after legal and social pressure.
- The **Fairtrade** movement aims to get businesses to pay suppliers in LEDCs a fair price for goods. The Co-op has taken an ethical stance on fairtrade — all its own brand chocolate is fairtrade.

Social and Environmental Influences

Environmental Issues create *Costs* and *Opportunities*

Pollution costs are mainly external costs i.e. they affect society, not the business itself.

1) Businesses pollute the environment through **production** processes, through **traffic pollution** caused by **transporting** raw materials and finished goods, through **dumping waste** in waterways and seas, and through **burying** or **burning waste**. **Packaging** creates a large amount of **landfill** waste.
2) External costs include health issues caused by air pollution, the greenhouse effect and acid rain.
3) Businesses also damage the environment through unsustainable resource management — e.g. cutting down rainforest for mining developments, building on greenfield sites.

Some costs of bad resource management are carried by the business itself.

1) Obviously, it makes **financial sense** to avoid wasting resources. Not using what you've paid for really wrecks those precious **cost-per-unit** ratios.
2) In the longer term, it makes sense to use resources **sustainably**. Completely **running out** of a resource would be bad news. Also, as resources **run low**, their **price rises** (supply and price are linked), increasing **costs**.
3) It's a good idea for businesses using **non-sustainable** resources to have **contingency plans**, so when the resource becomes too expensive or unavailable they will have other plans to fall back on.

Pollution control laws aim to pass the costs of pollution on to the business.

1) The government **fines** businesses who pollute more than a certain level. Pollution control is also done by **taxation**. This means that pollution has **internal financial costs.**
2) The **Environment Act (1995)** set up the **Environment Agency**, which coordinates pollution control. Businesses can't release pollution into waterways or land without a **permit** from the Environment Agency.
3) The EU directive on **Waste Electrical and Electronic Equipment (WEEE)** forces businesses to increase **recycling** of waste electrical and electronic equipment, much of which previously ended up in landfill sites.

Environmental issues create business opportunities as well.

1) Increased awareness of green issues creates **demand** for **environmentally friendly** products. For example, organic products command **higher prices**.
2) Because of increased awareness of environmental issues, and increased legislation about environmental issues, there's **demand for support services** to manage environmental control — e.g. consultancy and equipment.

Political Changes Affect Business

Domestic political changes, like a new government, affect business because they often result in a change to **economic policy**. Different political parties have different policies on issues such as how much businesses should be regulated.

Political change **abroad** can also affect business. For example, when the old Soviet Union and Eastern Bloc collapsed in the early 1990s, the economies of **Eastern Europe** opened up to trade with the West. This presented opportunities and threats to UK businesses.

Practice Questions

Q1 What are the responsibilities of a business towards its suppliers?

Q2 How can a business create goodwill in the local community?

Q3 What are business ethics?

Q4 Give an example of an opportunity created by environmentalism.

Exam Question

Q1 Evaluate the following statement: "Profit should be a higher priority than social responsibility for businesses". (14 marks)

All of a sudden, it's all fwuffy wuv...

Being all caring and sharing wouldn't seem to come naturally to businesses. It's a hard knock life, after all. A dog eat dog world, if you like. So, for a business to act ethically, there must be something in it for them. Learn the reasons why businesses might choose to act ethically.

Pressure Groups

Various pressure groups try to influence what businesses do.

Pressure Groups try to Influence government policies and business decisions

1) The aim of all pressure groups is to **influence** the people who have the **power** to **make decisions**.
2) There are pressure groups for all kinds of interests:

- **environmental** pressure groups such as Greenpeace and Friends of the Earth.
- **consumer** pressure groups such as the Consumer's Association.
- **animal welfare** pressure groups like the RSPCA and BUAV.
- **human rights** pressure groups such as Amnesty and Liberty.
- **business interest** pressure groups such as the CBI (Confederation of British Industry), who lobby the government to make laws more favourable to businesses.
- all **trade unions** are pressure groups.

Pressure Groups use Various Methods to Influence policies and decisions

Lobbying	Pressure groups discuss issues with **business decision makers** and **political decision makers**, to try to **influence** their thinking.
Direct action	Pressure groups organise **direct protests** against specific businesses (e.g. **boycotts** of Nestlé products, **blockades** of Shell petrol stations).
Publicity	Pressure groups try to make the **public** more **aware** of the issues. Consumers may **choose not to buy** a product which they think causes **social** or **environmental problems**.
Petitions	Petitions (lists of signatures) **prove** that people **agree** with the point of view of the pressure group.
Legal Action	Pressure groups can fight the firm through the **courts**, if they believe that the business is acting **illegally**.

Lobbying Politicians takes time

1) The aim of lobbying is to get politicians to word policies and laws the way you'd like them to be. It takes time for a pressure group to **win politicians around** to their point of view.
2) The first step for any pressure group is to put forward their issues and concerns to the lawmakers. Pressure groups do this by **writing letters** and holding **meetings**, and providing analysis and information.
3) Politicians are more likely to change the law if they think the new law will have **public support**, so it's important for pressure groups to do **publicity** campaigning at the **same time** as lobbying.

Direct Action against Businesses can be Very Powerful

1) Direct action can take the form of a **picketing** protest outside a factory or shop, an **organised boycott** of a product, a peaceful public protest, or even illegal **violent direct action** such as damage to property.
2) Businesses hate **negative publicity**. Direct protests by pressure groups bring unwanted publicity for the businesses, which may result in **lower sales**, or loss of **reputation**.
3) Direct action can also **prevent** the business from carrying out their **usual activities**.
4) Businesses weigh up the **costs** and **benefits** of giving in to direct action. They're more likely to give in when there's **widespread public support** for the pressure group, where the market is **competitive** enough that a boycott would hurt, and where their **public image** is seriously damaged by the protest.

Social Audits and Market Failure

Social Audits account for *Social* and *Ethical* performance

Sociable auditing.

1) A social audit assesses the **social impact** and **ethical behaviour** of a business in relation to **its aims** and those of its **stakeholders**. So, before performing a social audit, a business has to come up with **clear social objectives**. These include things like: choosing suppliers who don't use child labour, having a good health and safety policy, and using sustainable raw materials.
2) Social audits will look at the **social costs** of a business — the costs **society** has to bear because of the actions of a business. E.g. a firm dumps chemicals in a river, which is used by a town as a supply of drinking water. The town has to bear the costs of installing a special water treatment plant to counter the pollution.
3) The actual audit is done by an **independent external organisation**, just like a financial audit. They look at various **indicators** of performance, and they check up on what actually goes on inside the business.
4) The results of the audit are fed into the business's **strategic review** and planning processes, so that the business can make changes to improve social performance.

Environmental Auditing shows how a firm is affecting the *Environment*

1) An environmental audit is a review of the **environmental effects** of the firm's activities. It assesses whether the firm is meeting legal environmental protection requirements, and whether it's meeting it's own **targets**.
2) Environmental audits show businesses where they need to **change** their **resource management** and **waste management** practices.
3) For example, one of the environmental costs of business activity is the **greenhouse effect**. A business which has decided to **reduce** the amount of **greenhouse gases** emitted into the atmosphere would set a clear **objective** for reducing emissions, and **check their progress** towards this objective through an **environmental audit**.

Market Failure is when *Free Market* supply and demand *Don't Apply*

Free markets are supposed to **allocate resources** efficiently by the mechanism of supply and demand. Ideally, where there's a **demand** for a good, there'll be a **supply** to meet it — and supply and demand determine the **price** of the good.

Market failure occurs when free markets **don't** deliver an ideal **allocation of resources**, so supply doesn't meet demand. This can be when the good or service **can't** be provided by a free market of private suppliers because it's **impossible** to keep **non-buyers** from consuming it. It can also be when a monopoly charges **prices** which are too high.

Externalities cause market failure.

1) An externality is when the **outcome** of an economic action **isn't felt** by the person or business **responsible** — i.e. when the **social** costs and benefits don't match the **financial** costs and benefits.
2) For example, cancer is a **negative externality** caused by the consumption of tobacco. The government penalises tobacco manufacturers for this negative externality by charging higher tax rates on the sale of tobacco.
3) There are also **positive externalities**. For example, education and training benefit all of society. When a business invests in training, other businesses can benefit by employing the trained staff.

Practice Questions

Q1 What can governments do to deal with externalities?

Q2 Why do pressure groups lobby politicians?

Q3 Give an example of legal direct action.

Exam Questions

Q1 Analyse the government's policy of taxing tobacco products, particularly in terms of market failure. (14 marks)

Q2 Evaluate the methods that Greenpeace might use to stop supermarkets selling GM products. (16 marks)

I hope this isn't putting the squeeze on you...

Businesses don't operate in isolation from the rest of society. Their actions can impact on other people and the environment, which is why it's important they carry out different types of audit. Social and environmental audits are a way for businesses to assess how well they are performing in non-financial ways.

Impact of Change in Size

Growth causes a lot of changes to a business. It's not just that there are more people employed there — organisation may need to change, and a business may even take a different approach to long term planning.

Businesses can **Decide** whether to **Grow** or not

Growth doesn't happen by **accident**. It's up to the owners whether to **restrict growth** or **strategically plan** it. Business owners may choose to **restrict** growth for the following reasons:

1) They may want to **maintain the culture** of a small business.
2) If the business **over-markets** their products they could let customers down — the productive, administrative or distributive capacity may not be enough to handle the increased demand.
3) The business will become more **complicated** to manage as it gets bigger.
4) Growth requires the business to **secure additional financial resources**, which can be complicated.
5) They may not want to put too much **strain** on their **cash flow** position.

If the owners do decide that they want to **grow** the company, they must **devise a strategy** to **raise money** to pay for growth, and **plan** the growth process.

Growing Businesses must find sources of **Finance** — either internal or external

Whether the business finds it easy to attract the finance needed to grow will depend on a number of factors:

1) The **business plan** must be **realistic**, and must give an idea of when investors will see a return on their money.
2) The **previous reputation** of the business and its management affects how easy it is to borrow money.
3) The **type of ownership** of the business is a factor — e.g. whether it's a private or public limited company. A sole trader or partnership may have to become a **limited company**, so it can raise funds by selling shares.

Internal Finance comes from **Profits** or **Owners' Capital**

1) Sources of finance for growth depend on the **amount of capital** needed to implement the strategic growth plan. If the amount required is within the firm's own resources then expansion can be **funded internally**.
2) **Retained profits** (**trading profits**) are where the firm reinvests its profits back into its activities. This may work well as a firm expands from small to medium sized, but the funding available at any one time **could be too limited**.
3) **Owner's capital** is another source of growth funding. If the owners of the firm have the resources they could agree to **increase** their investment into the company. This source of funding is also limited.
4) **Selling assets** is another way a business can raise finance internally. They could sell the assets and then lease them back or sell assets that are no longer used. However, this is a one-off way of raising finance.
5) In most cases, firms need some **external investment** to fund their growth.

The way **External Funding** is raised depends on **Original Size** and **Ambitions**

1) If the business is relatively **small** or **medium sized** then the opportunities to raise finance are more **limited** than for a large or multinational company.
2) Established **smaller businesses** can raise finance through **loans from banks** but these may be **limited** to the purchase of new **capital equipment** or funding the opening of **new branches**.
3) If a small business has unlimited liability they'd be **unlikely** to attract external funding without becoming a limited company. This allows them to issue shares to raise capital. They may go to **venture capitalists** who would invest in the business for a limited period of time, say five years.
4) **Medium sized companies** could also convert from a private limited company to a **public limited company**. They could then raise finance through the **stock exchange** on the Alternative Investment Market (a stock market for medium size companies).
5) **Large** and **multinational businesses** are usually PLCs, already listed on the Stock Exchange, often in more than one country. They would be more likely to use a mixture of **substantial bank loans**, **rights issues** of shares (shares offered to existing shareholders at a discount), **sales of subsidiaries** and **retained profits** to fund growth.
6) Businesses can apply for **regional aid grants** if the expansion involves providing substantial additional employment in **deprived** areas.
7) **Debentures** are a type of **long term loan** businesses can use to raise finance. The loan has a fixed interest rate and the company has to offer some **collateral** to secure the loan. If the company can't repay the loan the collateral is sold to pay repay the lender.

Venture capitalists are people who invest in businesses for a living.

Impact of Change in Size

Growing Businesses *must manage their* **Cash Flow** *particularly carefully*

1) Just like at any other time, during a period of growth and investment it's essential that there are funds available to pay for the current **day-to-day expenses** of the business.
2) Fast growth increases the risk of **overtrading**. Increased **demand** means the business needs to buy more raw materials and employ more people. This **reduces** the amount of **working capital** available to pay the bills, and the business runs the risk that they'll go bust before they have the chance to get paid by their customers.
3) **Additional borrowing** may be required to manage working capital, which adds to the **costs** of the growth plan and therefore reduces the value added of the whole growth strategy.

Growing in Size *brings its* **Own Problems**

1) When a company changes from a **private limited company (Ltd)** to a **public limited company (PLC)**, the original owners won't find it so easy to maintain **control**, as they'll be responsible to a wider range of **shareholders**.
2) Once a company becomes a **PLC** then it's more open to being **taken over**. Anyone with sufficient resources could buy its shares in sufficient quantities to take a **controlling interest**.
3) Becoming a **PLC** can make managers more **short-termist**. Shareholders often want a **quick return** on investment through **dividend** payments, so they're **unlikely** to favour investment in **long-term projects**.
4) The process of **floating** the business on the **stock market** is **expensive** and **complicated**. The business would need to employ a **merchant bank** to apply for a stock market listing and handle the share offer for them. They'd need to use some of the finance raised to **fund** this.
5) When companies **expand overseas** they need to be familiar with the **commercial law** of the host country. They need to know the **employment regulations**, deal with the problems involved in carrying out transactions in **other currencies**, and comply with any regulations which cover the **product specifications** for those markets. Companies operating abroad may also have to deal with **different languages** and **cultures**.

Businesses *may become* **Smaller** *— this is called* **Retrenchment**

1) Businesses can choose to become smaller if they are suffering from diseconomies of scale.
2) They can **retrench** if they've lost focus. Doing too many different activities makes it hard to stay competitive.
3) Businesses can be forced to get smaller if they're **forced out of a market** by a larger competitor. They can also be forced to stop making some types of product by changes in **consumer taste**.
4) Also, changes in the **economy** such as recession or high interest rates may force a business to downsize.

Practice Questions

Q1 Why might a private limited company be reluctant to become a public limited company?

Q2 What is meant by the term "retained profits"?

Q3 Why is it important to manage cash flow during a transition period?

Q4 Why might a business take a short-term approach to planning after becoming a public limited company?

Q5 List five problems that a national business may have when it becomes an international business.

Q6 What is retrenchment?

Exam Question

Q1 Matthews Engineering Ltd., a private limited company, is a successful machine tools manufacturer. The Board has decided to open a factory in China as part of its strategic plan to expand into emerging markets. The set up costs will be substantial and the company will need to raise additional finance to fund it.

a) What problems should the Board be aware of when expanding overseas? (14 marks)

b) Evaluate the risks and benefits that the company faces as it implements this strategy. (18 marks)

Could a fertiliser business ever choose not to promote growth...

You need to know how businesses finance growth — which means revising some of the AS course. There are various potential problems that come with a change in size. Some of them are specific to mergers and takeovers, and they're covered on p.86-87. The rest of what you need to know is here.

Readjustment During Growth

When a business grows there's always a period of adjustment. Staff need to learn to work using different equipment, procedures and possibly in different teams.

Growth usually means that **Organisational Structures** have to **Change**

1) Most businesses start off as a **sole trader** or a partnership. These businesses are easy to manage — the **boss** can take all the **decisions**, and **organise** all the work.
2) As the business starts to grow, the boss **hires people** to help out. To start with, employee job descriptions can be quite **fluid**, and staff can take on tasks on an ad hoc basis (doing whatever's needed, whenever it's needed).
3) The next step is to move to a more **formal** structure. Employees are organised in **departments** under the control of a **department manager** and job descriptions become more **formal**. It's difficult for the boss to have control over the **whole organisation**, so some control is **delegated** to departmental managers.
4) As businesses get even larger, a simple formal hierarchy becomes an **ineffective** way of organising things, for the following reasons:
   - Often department managers work in **isolation** and don't know what's going on in other departments — e.g. sales departments may promise delivery dates which can't be met by production departments.
   - Management usually needs to **improve** the internal **communication** system to cope with this. There's a **danger** that businesses can become **over-bureaucratic** if they try to make communication foolproof. They can end up in a situation where **nobody's willing** to make a decision in a crisis because there's no **written permission** from above.
5) A boss who's been used to having **full authority** and control over large groups of employees, may have to learn how to become a **leader** or manager. **Senior managers** such as owner / manager or departmental managers who were **autocratic** by nature will have to learn to **trust** their subordinate employees. When a boss can't let go, and insists on knowing every little thing that's going on, the business can't grow very large.

During growth **Managers Delegate More**

1) As the business becomes more complicated, owners and managers have to **delegate** more tasks.
2) New **communications** systems are introduced to keep everyone in touch with what's going on. Departments must become less **isolated**. As tall hierarchies grow larger, communication chains get longer, which makes communication less effective.
3) Frequently the organisational structure will change from a **tall hierarchical structure** to a **flat** one (this is covered in the AS course). **Layers** of the hierarchy are removed, in a process called "delayering" (a bit of a predictable name). Senior managers take **responsibility** for **whole divisions** of the business — for example, a manager who was once responsible for only the production department may take responsibility for all aspects of producing and marketing a product.
4) There's often an emphasis on **teamwork**. It becomes the **responsibility** of teams to **manage** their work in such a way that they **meet targets** for quality, utilisation of equipment, customer service, training and budgeting.
5) Team leaders and managers can't be experts in all aspects of the processes involved, so they'll be expected to take **advice** from **subordinates** at whatever level they are employed.
6) Some businesses will encourage **Total Quality Management (TQM)** where all **operatives** are made **responsible for quality** at all stages of business activity. They are delegated the authority to remove a product from production lines if they notice a fault from the previous stage of production.
7) Businesses often take the opportunity to develop operational methods such as **kaizen**.

Managers Need Training to cope with growth

Even experienced managers may need **training** to learn how to effectively manage the changes that come with growth.

1) They need to be convinced that the changes are **necessary** so that they can explain them to subordinates.
2) It takes time for managers to **change attitudes** and learn to take a "hands off" approach to management, if they're used to an autocratic system.
3) Managing change in a business leads to **additional pressures** on managers and more work. **Time management** is an important skill to learn.
4) Managers will need to learn how to encourage subordinates to **contribute ideas** that may help improve the processes used in the firm.

Readjustment During Growth

Management must **Keep Control** of the growing business

1) As a business grows, and changes its organisational structure, it's **harder** for managers to **keep control** of what's going on.
2) In **flatter** structures, managers have **more subordinates** to manage, and they're ultimately responsible for **more activity**.
3) Larger businesses need good **planning systems**. **Budgeting** and **target setting** becomes particularly important.
4) **Management information systems** help managers keep **in touch** with day to day activities. All the relevant information is available to them, and they can call up any data they need.
5) **Management by objectives** helps businesses to **control** activities, and keeps everyone working towards the same **goals**.
6) **Formal appraisal** systems allow managers to keep tabs on what their staff are achieving.

Management by objectives is a management style that sets targets for everyone in a business, and then checks to see if they've met their targets.

Management must try to **Avoid** a **Loss** of **Direction**

1) During a period of growth and change it is management's responsibility to ensure that the **current aims and objectives** are met. For example, if service **falls short** of the standards expected by customers because of the organisational changes taking place, it's **no excuse** to say "Sorry you didn't receive your order and sorry that the new customer service staff didn't have a clue who you were. We're going through a period of growth and organisational change."
2) Staff must be **trained** into the new ways of working, to make sure that they all do things according to the new methods.
3) **Management by objectives** gives every single employee clear targets to meet, which are derived from the corporate goals. This makes sure that everyone is working towards the same goals, and going in the same direction.

An 18th century business strategy map.

Practice Questions

Q1 Explain how old working methods might become ineffective when businesses grow.

Q2 What is the difference between a hierarchical and flat organisational system?

Q3 What new skills would a manager with an autocratic style need to learn to encourage a team approach?

Q4 Why is it hard for managers to keep control of a growing business?

Q5 Why do communication systems become more complicated in a larger organisation?

Exam Question

Q1 During the restructuring of Castle Foods Limited, the Managing Director is concerned about the possible problems that could occur with one of the company's older managers. A firm of management consultants has identified that value added is falling in the production department. Delays are happening, as staff have been discouraged by the manager from doing anything without his authority. The manager has skills valuable to the company, and they do not want to lose his expertise.

a) Explain the type of management structure and leadership styles that have been used in Castle Foods before the restructuring. (14 marks)

b) What strategy do you think the Managing Director should follow to change the attitudes prevalent in the Production Department if it is to run efficiently after the restructuring? (16 marks)

Readjustment after growth — buy some new trousers that actually fit...

This all links neatly into the section on People in Organisations. Change management is needed after growth to cope with changes to the way the business is organised, including who reports to which manager, who has responsibility for quality, etc. It can be tough for managers to keep a growing business under control.

Change in Ownership

Changes in ownership of businesses can occur for several reasons and in several ways.

Changes of Ownership can be Takeovers or Mergers

Watch out with these terms, because they're often used incorrectly.

1) The definition of a **takeover** is when one business buys enough shares in another, so that they have more than 50% of the total shares. This is called a **controlling interest**, and it means the buyer will always win in a vote of all shareholders.
2) A **merger** happens when two companies **agree** that they should join together. To do this they have to **form** a company with a **new name**. The **shares** of this new company are then **transferred** to the shareholders of the old companies. There will be an agreement between the companies as to what these shares will be **worth** on the first day they are traded on the stock exchange.

Takeovers can be Agreed or "Hostile"

1) **Hostile takeovers** happen when one **public limited company (PLC)** buys a **majority** of the shares in **another** PLC. It can do this because the shares of PLCs are **traded** on the stock exchange and **anyone** can buy them. The company will encourage existing shareholders to sell them the shares by offering a good price for them. This is called a **premium**.
2) **Agreed takeovers** happen when shareholders or other types of owners such as sole traders **agree** that they'll sell the business to someone else. This is usually because the owners believe it would benefit the **survival** of the business.

There are Many Reasons why companies Take Over or Merge With others

1) Some businesses will decide to **diversify** and buy **existing** businesses operating in the **market they want to enter**. They **gain** from the **experience** of those employed by the businesses they buy, so they can **make profits faster**.
2) They may want to buy out companies that **operate in the same market** so that they can **reduce** the amount of **competition** that they face.
3) Other companies will want to **extend** their market in the **same industry** but in **other countries**. Examples of this: T-Mobile (a German mobile phone operator), bought One-to-One (a British mobile phone operator), France Telecom purchased Orange for the same reason.
4) Some large companies buy **suppliers** so they'll be sure that supplies won't be **disrupted**. They'll be able to **control** production of their supplies. This is becoming less common — large companies find it more **cost effective** to place **big contracts** with a **number** of suppliers. If there are **problems** with one they can use another.
5) Some businesses make profits from "**asset stripping**". They buy poorly performing businesses **cheaply** and then sell off the assets at a profit. The land on which the original business had its factory may be more valuable as building land, and could be **sold off** by the buyer at a nice profit.
6) Two large companies in the same industry may merge so that both could benefit from increased **economies of scale**. This is called **corporate integration**. In the car industry, companies such as Ford, Peugeot, BMW, and General Motors have bought out car manufacturers overseas. They can **switch production** from country to country where labour costs may be lower but the expertise already exists.

Takeovers and Mergers can be Horizontal, Vertical or Conglomerate

1) **Horizontal integration** happens when a firm buys out another firm in the **same industry**. It's the **most common** type of takeover or merger. It **reduces** the **competition** in the market. For example, the Morrisons supermarket chain bought out Safeways to extend its branch network and reduce competition.
2) **Vertical integration** occurs when a firm merges with or takes over another in the same industry but at a **different stage of the production process**.
3) Vertical integration can be **forward** or **backward**.

   Backward vertical integration is when a business buys its supplier.

   Forward vertical integration is when a manufacturer buys the **outlets** where its products are sold. This allows them **direct access** to the retail market. They can then **control** what is sold and exclude competitors' brands.
4) **Conglomerate mergers** are between **unrelated** firms — they aren't competitors of each other, and they aren't each other's supplier or customer. **Pure conglomerate mergers** are between totally unrelated firms. **Product extension mergers** are between firms making **related products** (e.g. hairbrushes and hairspray). **Geographic market extensions** are between firms in the same industry, but competing in **different geographic markets**.

Change in Ownership

Management Buy-Outs** are... when firms are bought by their **Managers

1) When the owners of the company want to **close** a division because it **no longer fits** in with its **strategic** plan (e.g. when a retailer no longer wants to own its suppliers) the managers of that division may buy it out.
2) When a company goes into **liquidation** because most of its subsidiaries are no longer profitable, the **liquidators** of the business may offer the management of a **profitable subsidiary** the opportunity to buy it.

Mergers, Takeovers** and **Buy-Outs** can be **Expensive

1) PLCs can **finance** the purchase of another company in several ways — retained profits, loans, share issues etc.
2) PLCs can act in partnership with other companies **in return** for a **shareholding** in the company they're buying.
3) They also get **private investment** from major shareholders through **rights issues**. This is where extra shares are issued and offered at a **reduced** price.
4) The potential buyer may buy shares from **existing shareholders** of the company. Often they have to buy them at a **premium** (a better price than the existing shareholders would get otherwise).
5) They might also make a **cash / share** offer where they pay cash for part of the share purchase and the rest of the price will be in the form of **shares in the new company**. With a cash / share offer, the buying company doesn't need to **raise** as much **finance** to complete the purchase.

Taking Over** other businesses is **Not Risk Free

1) Both businesses need to "learn to live with each other". There can be **tension** between staff of the merged businesses as they try to **establish** their **status** in the new organisation.
2) It will take **time** for staff to **learn** new procedures — **mistakes** could lead to **poor customer service**.
3) Some parts of the new organisation may need to be sold off or closed. This could mean additional **redundancy costs** which will **reduce profitability**.
4) When one business buys another, it **takes on all the liabilities** of the other business — this could include things like claims for long term disabilities suffered by ex-employees of the other business.
5) The **Competition Commission** investigate whether the proposed merger will **restrict competition** in the marketplace. If this is found to be the case the government can **stop** the takeover taking place or place **restrictions** on it. The finance used to **plan** a merger or takeover would then be **wasted**.
6) If a takeover is part of a **diversification strategy**, the purchasing business will have **limited experience** in the new industry and it will take time to **learn** how it works. Mistakes would **reduce profitability**.

Practice Questions

Q1 When would you consider a takeover to be "hostile"?

Q2 What's the difference between a takeover and a merger?

Q3 Why do you think a company would encourage a management buy-out?

Q4 What is the most common type of integration when a large company buys a similar company in the same industry?

Q5 What's "asset stripping"?

Q6 What is the difference between vertical and horizontal integration?

Exam Question

Q1 A high street fashion retailer is concerned that the overall group profits are falling yet turnover is up. The Board of Directors receive a report from their management consultants which indicates that the problem is one of rising costs. There have been delays in receiving deliveries from suppliers due to delays at the supplier's factories. After some discussion the Board decides that they should buy two of their suppliers, both of which are small PLCs.

a) Why do you believe that the Board took this decision? (14 marks)

b) Evaluate the risks involved in taking this approach. (18 marks)

Don't get confused between takeovers and mergers...

Here's yet another page on growth and change management. This one's about mergers, takeovers and buy-outs, which are a topic on their own. You know, I can't quite decide whether "backwards vertical integration" sounds rude or not...

Organisational Culture and Strategy

Organisational culture, sometimes called corporate culture, affects the way a business sets its objectives.

Mission Statements are Written Statements of Corporate Aims

1) **Mission statements** are written **descriptions** of corporate aims. They set out what the business does, why they do it, and how they're going to go about providing the best customer service.
2) Mission statements are intended to make all **stakeholders** aware of the corporate aims, and to **encourage** all employees to **work towards** them. Businesses sometimes involve staff from **all levels** of the hierarchy in formulating the statement. Everyone in the business should know what the mission statement **means**, **agree** with it, and know how **they** can contribute to "make it so".
3) Mission statements need to be **reviewed** from time to time to make sure they don't go out of date. **Changes** in the external business environment can mean that the business needs to adjust its mission statement.
4) Mission statements are sometimes **criticised** because they cost a lot of money and management time to create. To be worthwhile, a mission statement must give **benefits** that **outweigh the costs of writing it**.
5) Sometimes mission statements are only **publicity tools**, with no real substance behind them. Remember, the effectiveness of a mission statement depends on what it gets people to do, not on the fancy words it uses.

Once the Mission Statement is decided, the business can Set its Objectives

Corporate objectives are **quantifiable**. Remember, objectives should be **SMART**, which stands for **S**pecific, **M**easurable, **A**greed, **R**ealistic and **T**ime-specific.

Specific objectives set out **exactly** what the business **intends to achieve**.

Measurable objectives make it easy to **monitor progress**.

Agreed objectives get more **commitment** from employees than objectives handed down from on high.

Realistic objectives are achievable. There's **no point** in having objectives you can't meet.

Time-specific objectives give a deadline to **aim** for.

Organisational Culture is the Way a business Does Things

1) **Organisational culture** is the way that a business does things, and the way that people in the business expect things to be done. It shapes the **expectations** and **attitudes** of staff and managers.
2) Because organisational culture **shapes staff behaviour** and how they make decisions, it has an effect on planning, objective setting and strategy.
3) Organisational culture is created and reinforced by company **rules**, **managerial attitudes** and behaviour, **recruitment** policies that recruit people who "fit in", **reward** systems (e.g. how bonuses are calculated and allocated), and "**ceremonies**" such as office **parties**.
4) Businesses can have underlying cultures within **departments**, known as **subcultures**. For example, a design department might be relaxed, whereas the head of sales might run a very tight ship.
5) Organisational culture is **really difficult to change** once it's established. People get set in their ways. Changing organisational culture doesn't **only** mean changing **processes** and **objectives** (which is hard enough, let's be honest). It means changing what people **believe** about the business and their role in it.

Mission Statements give Clues to corporate culture

1) Mission statements give **clues** about culture. For example, a mission statement that mentions ethics and principles gives a big hint that the corporate culture is focused towards ethical practice as well as profitability.
2) Some mission statements **explicitly** state what the business believes its corporate culture is. After a short statement of corporate aim and vision for the future, there may be an actual **statement of shared beliefs**, e.g. "We believe in providing outstanding service to customers", "We believe that we gain strength through our diversity".
3) Mission statements try to create a **unifying**, visible culture for all employees to **identify** with. This helps prevent the business fragmenting into too many different subcultures.
4) **Changing** the mission statement can help change corporate culture.

Organisational Culture and Strategy

*There are **Four Main Types** of **Organisational Culture***

1) **Power culture** refers to organisations where decision-making authority is limited to a **small number** of people —perhaps just **one person**.
2) In these businesses, objectives reflect the wishes of the guy or gal at the **top**.

1) **Role culture** refers to **bureaucratic** firms where authority is defined by job title.
2) These organisations tend to **avoid risk** for fear of failure so they develop **cautious** aims and objectives.
3) The danger here is that over-cautious companies can lose out in the long run, especially in **new** or **expanding** markets where strategies need to be developed and implemented quickly. Organisations with role culture often fail to exploit opportunities before their competitors do.

1) **Person culture** refers to loose organisations of individual workers, usually **professional partnerships** such as solicitors.
2) The objectives of these firms will be defined by the **personal ambitions** of the individuals involved. Care is needed to ensure individuals actually have **common goals**.

1) **Task culture** places an emphasis on tasks and **getting things done**.
2) Task culture gets **small teams** together to work on a project, then disbands them. There may be **conflict** between teams for resources and budgets. This can led to confusion if a firm has too many products or **projects**.
3) This culture supports objectives which are based around **products** (e.g. make Product X the market leader).
4) Task cultures respond well to **management by objectives**. Management by objectives translates corporate objectives into **specific targets** for each **department** and for each **individual employee**.

__Organisational Culture__ is linked to __Management Styles__

1) The **power** culture matches up with the **autocratic** style. An autocratic leader doesn't like to let anyone else have responsibility for making decisions, let alone setting corporate objectives.
2) The **role** culture can be linked to a **paternalistic** style of leadership. It's not compatible with a fully democratic style of leadership, because big bureaucratic firms aren't good enough at communication to consult and delegate decision-making.
3) The **person** culture is linked to a **laissez-faire** style of leadership. The workers are generally individual **professionals** and can be **trusted** to make their own decisions and generally **get on with it** by themselves.
4) The **task** culture is linked to a **democratic** style of leadership, with **delegation** of responsibility. Teams working on tasks need the responsibility to make their own decisions, and the freedom to organise themselves in the way they think best, in order to meet corporate objectives.

Practice Questions

Q1 What is organisational culture?

Q2 Describe the power culture, and its approach to setting objectives.

Q3 Which culture is best suited to management by objectives?

Q4 Which culture is linked to the democratic style of management?

Exam Question

Q1 Filton Electronics is a medium size manufacturer of diodes. Until recently, it was run by owner Jim Filton and a small team of department managers, in a strict functional hierarchy. It has been taken over by a firm who practise Japanese management methods such as kaizen, JIT production, teamworking and quality circles. The parent firm's mission statement says "we will improve our standards every day, and communicate excellence throughout the business". Suggest changes that Filton must make to their organisational culture, and explain why they should be made. (14 marks)

Look for clues about culture...

In the exam you'll have a case study of a business, and you could be asked about strategy, staff motivation, external influences or organisational culture. The case study will be full of clues about the culture — it'll probably tell you a story of how the managers acted in a particular situation rather than saying "this firm has a TASK culture".

Decision-Making Models

There are a number of decision-making tools used by managers to help them determine the most profitable business strategy.

Decision-Making is essential to Planning

A business plan is a **collection of decisions** about what to do. Without decision-making, you can't make a plan.

Senior managers make **strategic decisions** to set the **long term direction** of the business.

Junior managers make **tactical decisions** about how to implement the strategy on a day-to-day basis.

Decisions can be made Scientifically — or based on Hunches

Scientific decision-making means **collecting** data, **analysing** it to arrive at a **conclusion** and then **testing** that decision to see if it works.

The **alternative** to the scientific approach is **inspired guesswork** based on **experience** or **gut reaction**.

Various factors influence how managers make decisions

1) The **type** of problem is a factor — it could be a **routine** problem or a **one-off situation**. Routine problems can be handled with an experience-based approach. **Unfamiliar** problems call for research and analysis.
2) The **personality** of the decision-maker is a factor — some people are better at accepting risk than others.
3) The **decision-maker's job** might be in danger if they get the decision wrong, or the **survival** of the business might be on the line. The **bigger the decision**, the more likely a manager is to do plenty of **research** first. This is common sense stuff if you think about it.
4) Decisions that can be **easily changed** can be made by educated guesswork. Decisions that can't be reversed are by definition more **risky**. They need some serious thought.

1) You've probably looked at some methods used in scientific decision-making before, e.g. **break-even analysis** (p.30-31) and **investment appraisal** (p.34-37).
2) Most methods of scientific decision-making are **costly** and **time-consuming**, but they **reduce** the risk of making **expensive mistakes**.
3) Research methods used are highly dependent on the **quality** of the data collected.
4) The **quantity** of data has an affect too. Given a limited amount of information, most people make a good, reasoned decision. When there's too much data (**information overload**) a lot of it's ignored.

Businesses analyse their Current Situation using SWOT

A business's strategic analysis model should deal with the **internal** and **external** environment. Managers use SWOT analysis to help determine strategy. **SWOT** is a kind of **situational audit** — it tells managers **where the business is** in terms of its strengths and weaknesses, and the opportunities and threats that the market currently offers.

1) The business must look at itself to identify its **strengths** and **weaknesses**. An internal audit must be **factual** and **objective** — wishful thinking isn't helpful.
2) The **external** environment provides the **opportunities** the business wants to exploit and the **threats** that might prevent success.
3) SWOT lets the business know where it has a **competitive advantage** over its rivals.

Strengths
Weaknesses
Opportunities
Threats

PEST analysis shows what's going on Outside The Business

The **PEST** model is used to complete the external audit of opportunities and threats. PEST stands for **P**olitical, **E**conomic, **S**ocial and **T**echnological factors — things which can influence the way the business operates.

1) **Political** factors include **legal** and **fiscal** ones too, for example, changes in laws, customs duty on goods, taxation levels and, of course, changes of government.
2) **Economic** factors include **inflation**, **budget changes**, rising oil prices and **unemployment**.
3) **Social** or **cultural** factors cover **lifestyle changes**, **educational reform**, **environmental changes** and **population movement**. These affect the consumers of the product or service, and the labour market.
4) **Technology** is constantly changing as new materials and products are invented and energy saving substitutes and production methods are introduced.

Decision-Making Models

Marketing Decision-Making usually uses a Scientific Approach

1) The **scientific marketing model** consists of a series of **stages**: setting **objectives**, **gathering data**, **analysing** data, forming a **hypothesis** (a **marketing strategy**), **testing** it out to see if it works, and **changing** it if necessary.
2) **Market research** is **fundamental** — it's impossible to form a hypothesis or test it without **good data**.

See p.8 for more about scientific marketing.

Marketing also uses decision-making Models

Several tools are used by marketing managers to help them **adapt** to changing situations and develop **new strategies**.

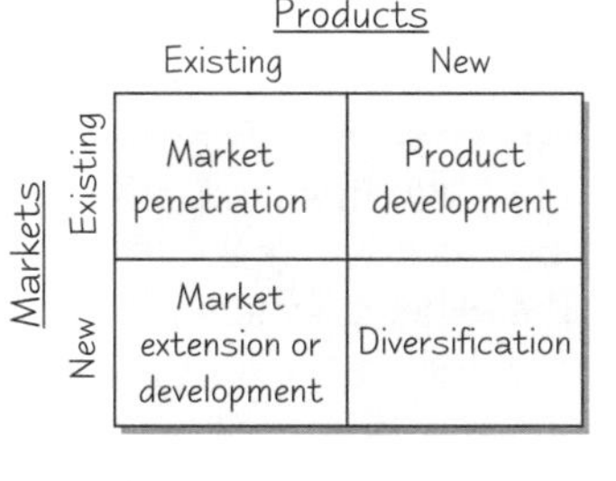

1) Market analysis tools like **Ansoff's Matrix** (p.9) help to evaluate the comparative risk of differing strategies.
2) The **AIDA model** for advertising sets out four stages that advertising communication should go through to ensure the customer makes the important decision to purchase. See p.8.
3) The **DAGMAR model** sets out five stages that consumers move through when buying a product, from unawareness through awareness, comprehension, and conviction to action. See p.9.

AIDA = Attention, Interest, Desire, Action.

DAGMAR = Defining Advertising Goals for Measured Advertising Results .

Other Departments use Scientific Decision-Making

1) **Operations managers** analyse and evaluate **productivity data**. They use various **planning tools** to improve the decision–making process to achieve higher efficiency and quality — e.g. **Critical Path Analysis** (see p.60-61) and **product life cycles** and **Decision Trees** (see p.92-93).
2) Accountants and financial managers analyse **financial data** and performance measures to develop the business's financial plans. They use **investment appraisal** techniques, **ratio analysis**, **budgeting**, variances and **break-even** (see p.30-31).
3) Human Resources managers use data on workforce needs, availability and training costs / benefits in their **workforce planning**. They use **performance measures** to analyse the success of their activities.

Practice Questions

Q1 Explain how the decision-making process can be influenced by the decision-maker's personality.

Q2 What four things does PEST analysis tell managers about the market situation?

Q3 What four things does SWOT analysis tell businesses about their current situation?

Exam Question

Q1 Look Lovely Ltd is a small player in the UK cosmetics market. In the past ten years it has concentrated its sales efforts on its mail order business. The aim was to reduce distribution costs and sell products at lower prices. A website has also been developed. The current product range includes a budget range of cosmetics aimed at the teenage market and an "anti-ageing" skin care range aimed at older customers. A business consultant's report commented that the firm, "must grow just to maintain its position in the changing, highly competitive cosmetics market," and recommended that it should, "broaden its distribution channels" or "introduce new product ranges".

a) Prepare a SWOT analysis for Look Lovely Ltd. (14 marks)

b) How can Ansoff's Matrix be relevant to solving Look Lovely Ltd's lack of growth problem? (16 marks)

c) What other information, apart from financial data, would you require to assess the likelihood of Look Lovely Ltd surviving in the UK cosmetics market? Justify your selection of data. (16 marks)

When you can't decide, just ask a model. They know a lot...

Decision-making models can help with any business decision, whether it's to do with marketing, production, human resources or whatever. SWOT and PEST are the basic one-size-fits-all ways of working out what the situation is — after that, managers still have to come up with the best plan. Experience can be extremely useful alongside the scientific approach.

Decision Trees

Decision trees are a mathematical model used for decision making, incorporating probability.

Decision Tree Analysis combines Probability and Expected Benefit

The outcome of any decision is rarely guaranteed — it might NOT happen. Decision tree analysis is used in business to balance the **probability** of an event occurring against the **expected reward**.

1) **Probability** is the **likelihood** of an event occurring. Some probabilities are known for certain, like the flip of the coin which is 50% probability of heads, 50% tails. If a probability is unknown an **estimate** is made by managers based on **experience** or **past data** — this estimate is **subjective**.
2) **Expected Value** is the **probability** of an event occurring, **multiplied** by the **benefit** the business can expect to gain. For example, a business launching a new product wants to decide whether to invest £100,000 in an advertising campaign. The campaign has a 0.7 chance of success. If the campaign is a success it will make £200 000. However, if it fails (with a probability of 0.3) it will make only £20 000. The expected value is therefore 0.7 × 200 000 + 0.3 × 20 000 = £146 000. In this case this is higher than the cost of the campaign (£100 000). So the campaign should be done.

Learn these Features of Decision Trees

1) A **square** represents a **decision point**.
2) **Circles** (or **nodes**) mark where there are **alternative outcomes**, which are shown by **lines** coming out of the node.
3) The **decimals** on the lines are the **probabilities** of each event occurring.
4) The **values in £s** represent the **income** to the business if that outcome happens.

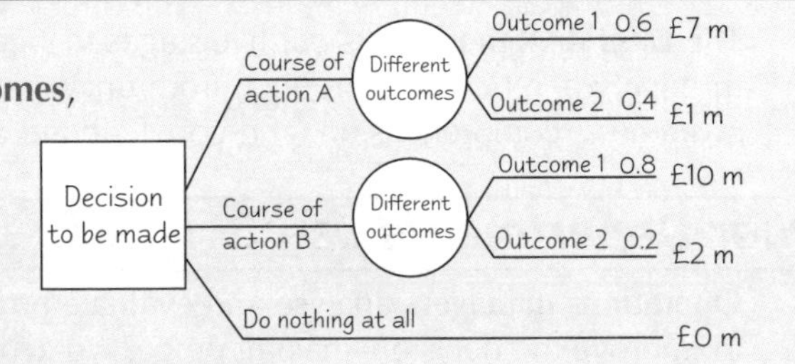

Decision Trees show which Course Of Action is Best

1) When creating a decision tree, managers first identify which courses of action are open to the business.
2) They then outline the **possible results** of each course of action.
3) They assign **probabilities** to each of the results — filling in the probabilities they know for certain, and estimating the probabilities they don't know.
4) The next step is to **calculate** the "**expected values**" of each result.
5) Managers choose the course of action with the **highest expected value**.

Case Study — Decision Tree for Launching a New Product

A business wants to **launch a new product**.

1) **With a market research budget of £15K** the chance of a **successful launch** is estimated at **75%**.
2) **Without market research** the chance is estimated at **50%**.
3) A **successful** launch would earn a profit of **£100K** — but if it **failed**, profit would be **£20K** at best.

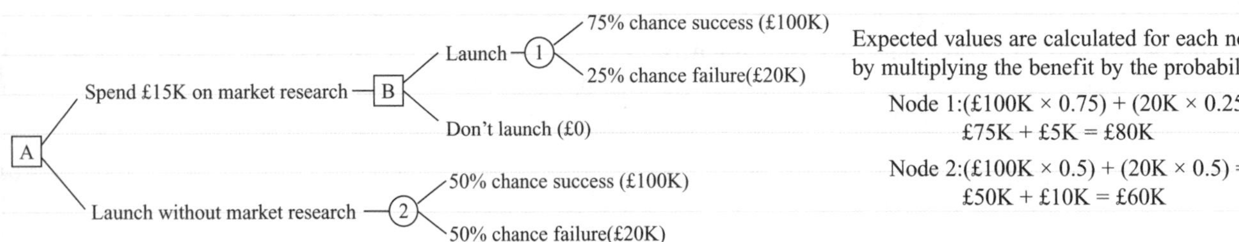

Expected values are calculated for each node point by multiplying the benefit by the probability:

Node 1:(£100K × 0.75) + (20K × 0.25) = £75K + £5K = £80K

Node 2:(£100K × 0.5) + (20K × 0.5) = £50K + £10K = £60K

Compare the decisions — the decision at square B is the most straightforward, so start with that one.

Square B The decision at square B is whether to launch or not. Compare the **expected value of the launch** (**£80K**) with **not launching** (**£0**). After market research, it's best to go ahead with the launch.

Square A To **compare like with like**, take off the **cost of market research** from the expected value of launching after market research. This works out as £80K – £15K = **£65K**. Compare this amount with the expected value of launching without any research, which is £60K. So, it's better to do the research than to not do the research.

So, the final decision is... to **launch after carrying out market research**.

Decision Trees

Decision Trees have Advantages...

1) Decision tree analysis makes managers **work out** and **think about** the **probability** of each outcome, and the **potential payoff** of each outcome. Managers have to come up with real numerical values for these — much better than vague statements like "this will increase sales".
2) Decision trees are a nice **visual representation** of the potential outcomes of a decision.
3) Decision trees allow managers to compare options **quantitatively** and **objectively**, rather than plumping for the fashionable option or the option they thought of first.

...and Disadvantages

A business should never rely on one single tool as the basis for determining its long term strategy.

1) Decision trees are **quantitative** — i.e. they're numerically based. There's a wide range of non-numerical **qualitative data** which a business must take into account before deciding on a course of action.
2) **Probabilities** are very hard to **predict accurately**. **Estimated payoffs** are also assumed to be accurate — in real life things may work out differently. If either of these estimates are based on **dodgy** information, the decision is **flawed** too.
3) In reality there's a **wider range** of potential **outcomes** than the decision tree suggests. For example, a new marketing campaign might increase sales for a shorter period than predicted — the decision tree might only allow for success or failure, not for short-term success versus long-term success.

Practice Questions

Q1 Explain the difference between the circles (nodes) and the squares on a decision tree.

Q2 Outline the five stages used in decision tree construction.

Q3 Define expected value and say how it's calculated.

Q4 Give one disadvantage of decision tree analysis.

Exam Question

Q1 Cruse plc is a multinational electronic defence systems organisation. It has won a contract to overhaul the electronics on an ex-Royal Navy submarine. Three other submarines require similar work in the next four years but Cruse plc does not have the current capacity to complete these contracts in the time available. To win the subsequent contracts Cruse has three options: increase capacity, use existing resources but take longer, or subcontract two-thirds of the work. Expected outcomes are as follows:

Option	Outcomes	Probability	Profit (£m)
Increase existing capacity	Success	0.4	700
	Slight success	0.5	400
	Failure	0.1	-100
Use existing capacity	Success	0.4	400
	Slight success	0.3	200
	Failure	0.3	-30
Subcontract	Success	1	300

Answer on p.98.

(a) On the basis of the information given, construct a decision tree for this problem and label it showing probabilities and forecast pay-offs. (14 marks)

(b) Calculate the expected value for each option. Advise Cruse as to the best option. (14 marks)

(c) Assess the usefulness of constructing a decision tree in this case. (14 marks)

(d) Discuss other factors which Cruse plc might consider when taking the decision. (18 marks)

An oak and a fir go into a bar, and the barman says "so, what'll it be"...

Decision trees are a really nifty way of working out what the best option is, when a manager is faced with an important decision. It's based on the potential benefit if things work out well, and the likelihood of it working out well or badly. Practise working your way through a few decision trees to get the hang of it — don't leave it all until the day of the exam.

Corporate Plans

Corporate plans (business plans) are long term plans which help the business pursue its objectives.

Decisions can be either Strategic or Tactical

1) A **strategy** is a **long-term plan** for how to achieve **objectives**. For example, an **objective** of **increasing profits** can be achieved by a **strategy** of **reducing costs**.
2) **Tactics** are the actual **activities** that a firm uses to implement its strategy. For example, a **strategy** of **reducing costs** could be implemented by the **tactic** of changing to a **cheaper supplier**.

Strategic decisions	Tactical decisions
Long-term decisions about **what strategy to follow**.	**Short-term** decisions about how to **implement** the strategy.
Involve a high level of **uncertainty**.	Involve less **uncertainty**.
Large **commitment** of **resources**.	Less **resources committed**.
Difficult to reverse.	Easier to change.
Usually made by **senior management**.	Can be made by **less senior staff**.

For example: the decision to invest in building a new production facility is a **strategic** decision — it's a decision about a firm's **strategy**, it'll take a lot of **resources** (time, money and effort), and it's very **hard to scrap the decision** half way through implementing it.

The decision to use carpet tiles for the office flooring in the production facility is a **tactical** decision. It doesn't have to be made months in advance, and it can be easily changed.

Businesses make Corporate Plans which set out their overall strategy

1) Corporate plans set out **objectives** for the business as a whole, and set out the **overall strategy** the business will use to reach its objectives.
2) For example, a corporate plan lays out how the business intends to **survive**, whether the business intends to **grow**, and **how** they might go about growing.
3) The corporate plan will also include an outline of goals for each department. The **fine details** are set out in individual departmental plans.
4) Management aim to have all the parts of the business **working together** towards a **goal**. The idea is that the **combined** effort of **everyone together** is **greater** than the **sum** of everyone's individual efforts. This "whole is greater than the sum of the parts" idea is sometimes called **synergy**.

Businesses produce Strategic Plans for All Areas of their activity

The corporate plan is a long term strategic plan, which doesn't contain all the **fine detail** different departments of the business need. Plans for all the different departments of the business are derived from the overall corporate plan.

1) **Marketing plans** set out **marketing objectives**, and say **how** the business is going to meet its objectives. They give details of **new products**, **new markets**, and **strategies** to increase market share. The marketing plan says how much money will be **spent** on marketing activities, and how much money marketing activities will be expected to **bring in**.
2) **Human Resource plans** set out HR objectives and strategy. They describe how human resources will be **actively managed** to help the business meet its **corporate objectives**. Human resources plans state how **big** the workforce needs to be, and what **skills** they need to have. They set out policies to make sure that the workforce meets the needs of the business — e.g. recruitment plans and training plans.
3) **Production plans** set out the **level of production** that the business needs in order to meet its corporate objectives. The business must produce the **right quality** of goods, as **quickly** and **cheaply** as possible.
4) **Financial plans** set out how much **money** is expected to flow **into** and **out of** the business. Financial plans include the **cash flow forecast**, and **projections** of what the **balance sheet** and **profit and loss** statement will look like.

Corporate Plans

A Strategy is Not For Life — it must be continually Checked and Reviewed

1) It's very important that the managers who devise a strategy also **monitor** it for **effectiveness**. There needs to be **constant monitoring** of whether all the parts of the business (marketing, production and human resources) are **meeting** the targets they've been set. If they aren't, then it's essential to find out why not.
2) When producing the plan, the organisation will include a series of **planning horizons**. This is the time scale by when each part of the plan will be met. The **financial objectives** will be set and the actual performance will be measured against a **forecast** made at the start of the planning cycle.
3) The results may not be meeting expectations. A **difference** between a strategic target and reality is called a **strategic gap**. By **analysing** the gap, managers can find out **why** there is a difference between the target and the reality, and take corrective action.

Even the Best Laid Plans of (mice and) Managers can Go Wrong

The business environment is **changing** all the time. External and internal changes can mess things up — they mean that a good plan suddenly isn't so good any more.

1) Changes in **technology** can **increase the productivity** of **competitors**. Changes in technology can make a product **obsolete**.
2) **Consumer tastes** can change **quickly**, which reduces the length of the product life cycle.
3) Improvements in **communications** systems can benefit competitors. Businesses may feel forced to make changes to keep up with competitors — e.g. by outsourcing customer services to India or other low labour cost countries.

Contingency Plans prepare for Out Of The Ordinary Events

Corporate plans plan for the **expected**. Unfortunately, **unexpected events** can throw a spanner in the works.

Example: Most businesses have a **contingency plan** in case of **IT** disasters. For example, they might take **backups** of their data at the end of each day. Some of these backups must be **stored off-site** — otherwise if there was a fire at the site, all the data would be lost, even the backups. That would be very sad, and very, very expensive.

1) When you're evaluating a firm's plans for the future, make sure they have some kind of **contingency plan**.
2) Remember, though, that no business can plan for **every unforeseen event**. Some adverse events are hard to plan for. It could actually **cost the business less** to let them happen than it would cost to **plan** for them.
3) Managers must decide **how likely** a particular adverse event is to happen, and how **badly** it would damage the business if it did happen.
4) Contingency planning means **constantly questioning assumptions** about what's going to happen.

Practice Questions

Q1 What might be included in a human resource plan?

Q2 What are contingency plans for?

Q3 What would you expect to find in a corporate plan?

Q4 What is the purpose of a business plan to an expanding company?

Exam Questions

Q1 Pancho Toys Ltd wants to expand its business and has drawn up an appropriate business plan to attract potential investors. Evaluate the criteria you would use to judge whether or not to buy shares in Pancho Toys. (14 marks)

Q2 Suggest the likely contents of a supermarket's contingency plan to cope with a potential lorry drivers' strike. (14 marks)

Get with the plan, people...

Remember that this section is tested in a "synoptic" paper that gets you to apply strategic thinking to any area of the A level syllabus — organisational structure, human resources, marketing strategy, production methods, etc. So, you've got to think about themes that have come up in other sections of the book, and in the AS course, while you learn this lot.

Do Well in Your A2 Exam

*This page is about what you're **actually marked on** in A2 Business Studies exams.*

You get marks for **AO1 (showing knowledge)** and **AO2 (applying knowledge)**

AO1 marks are for **content** and **knowledge**. You'll only get about 2 marks for this, whether the question is a short one worth 2 marks, shortish one worth 6 marks or a long one worth 15 marks. At A2 level, they assume you know the facts.

AO2 marks are for **applying** your **knowledge** to a **situation** — e.g. thinking about the type of ownership of the business in the question, the product or service it's selling, the type of market it's in. You usually get 2-3 marks for this as well.

You get marks for **AO3 (analysis)** and **AO4 (evaluation)**

AO3 marks are for **analysis** — thinking about benefits, drawbacks, causes, effects and limitations. Analysis questions usually start with words like "**Analyse**", "**Examine**", "**Explain why**" or "**Consider**".

1) Use your knowledge to **explain** your answer and **give reasons**.
2) With data, say what the figures **mean**, what might have **caused** them and what the **consequences** might be.
3) Write about **context** — compare a business' situation with the industry as a whole, or with a competitor.

AO4 marks are for **evaluation** — using your **judgement**. Evaluation questions usually start with words like "**Evaluate**", "**Discuss**", "**Recommend**" or "**To what extent**".

1) Give **two sides** of an argument, and say which you think is **strongest**. Consider **advantages** and **disadvantages** and weigh them up.
2) You don't need a definite answer. You can point out that it depends on various factors — as long as you say what the factors are, and say why the right choice depends on those factors. Use your **judgement** to say what the **most important factors** are.
3) Relate your answer to the **business described in the question** and to the **situation in the question**. Give reasons why the business would make a particular decision, and how and why the particular circumstances might affect their decision.

A2 Material is **Based** on **AS Material** — your **AS Work** is **Relevant**

Even though you're taking the A2 exams, you'll still be expected to **use information you learned** during the AS course:

1) As **background knowledge** to help you **apply knowledge**, and **analyse** and **evaluate** business decisions.
2) As part of a "**synoptic**" paper which tests knowledge from the AS part of the course as well as the A2 part.

Some of the A2 course covers the **same material** as the AS course, but in more detail, or from a slightly different angle.

You get marks for **Quality** of **Written Communication** in essays and coursework

1) You have to write a **well-structured essay**, not a list of bullet points.
2) You need to use **specialist vocabulary** when it's appropriate, so it's worth **learning** some of the **fancy terms** used in this book.

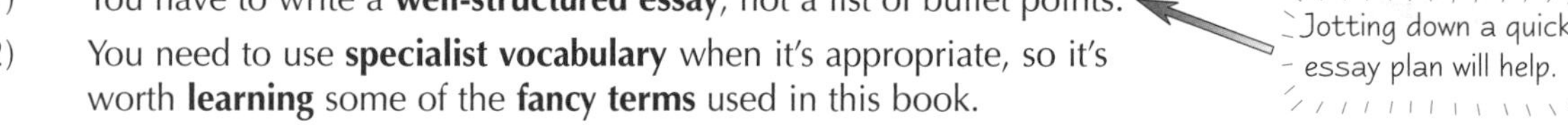

3) Write **neatly** enough for the examiner to be able to read it and use good **spelling**, **grammar** and **punctuation**. Out of the whole paper, you only get **2** or **3** marks for written communication — but remember that if the examiner can't **read** or **understand** your writing, you won't get the **other marks** either.

All the **Skills** are **Marked Separately**

For example, an **evaluation** question has some AO1 marks for **content**, some AO2 marks for **application**, some AO3 marks for **analysis** and some AO4 marks for **evaluation**.

- You can **lose marks** for poor content, application and analysis.
- If you evaluate possible pros and cons **without** specifically stating the **obvious facts**, and specifically **relating** them to the **actual business situation** in the question, you'll **lose out**.

There are still more marks for analysis and evaluation than for basic facts, though.

Do Well in Your A2 Exam

There are three *Exam Units* at A2

1) There are **three examinations** at A2 — units 4, 5 and 6. **Units 4** and **5** are both worth **15%** of the total A level marks. **Unit 6** is worth **20%**. Each examination lasts **90 minutes**.
2) **Unit 4** is based on a Case Study. It assesses **Module 4** (Marketing and Accounting and Finance) and **Module 5** (People and Operations Management). The questions on Unit 4 are **compulsory** and require you to analyse written information and numerical data.
3) **Unit 5** assesses **all three A2 modules** and comprises two sections. **Section A** usually has a single compulsory question worth **40 marks**. It gives you data in the form of tables, charts and lists and requires you to write a report justifying a business decision. **Section B** normally contains four long essay questions. You must answer **one question** which is again worth **40 marks**. If you have submitted coursework for this unit you won't have to sit the exam.
4) **Unit 6** is also based on a **Case Study** (given to you in the paper). It assesses **Module 6** (**External Influences and Objectives and Strategy**). The current pattern is for five questions, each worth **14-18 marks**. **Unit 6** is called the "**synoptic**" paper, which means it assesses your ability to build an argument by drawing from your knowledge about **all parts** of the **specification**. So, for unit 6 you need to revise everything, not just the External Influences and Objectives and Strategy stuff.

Here's an *Example Essay* to give you some *Tips*

To what extent is marketing irrelevant to a manufacturer supplying nails to the construction industry? (10 marks)

Don't waffle. Start by making a point.

Marketing is the management process responsible for identifying, anticipating and satisfying the needs of customers profitably.

This is straight to the point. It picks up "knowledge" marks straight away.

There are two markets in which a business can sell its product, one being the consumer market and the other the industrial market. Constant changes within consumer markets make it vital for businesses to undertake market research when deciding upon a possible new product or when analysing the success of their existing product. Marketing is therefore very important.

This shows understanding and develops an argument that's carried on in the next paragraph.

Nails could be classified as product-orientated and are more commonly sold in the industrial market. Because the industrial market for building materials is not subject to differing trends and fashions, one could argue whether marketing is as important as in consumer markets. Nails are commodities that are not affected by changing fashions or consumer attitudes. Because of this I feel marketing is to some degree of little use.

This gets some analysis (A03) and evaluation (A04) marks.

Above the line promotion is an important aspect of the marketing mix in consumer markets. However, for industrial markets below the line promotions are more important and customers are more likely to be concerned about specification, functionality, delivery and price than image. Marketing concentrates on satisfying the consumer's needs. With this in mind, I would say that marketing is important to a nail manufacturer, as it will provide them with knowledge of the economy. For example a decrease in interest rates will prompt people to take out loans and engage in home projects such as conversions or extensions; this would lead to an increase in the demand for nails from wholesalers or large retail chains. Additionally, marketing will be useful in analysing competitive prices and specifications.

Good points, but not explained well enough.

This is good application of knowledge to the business in the question.

I would conclude, therefore, that marketing is of relevance to a nail manufacturer, although not all aspects will be as important as others.

You should put in a conclusion to sum up your argument. This one is a bit weak.

This is a good answer. It would get about **8 marks**. The candidate has a good understanding of the nature of marketing within industrial markets and has demonstrated the ability to **analyse** and **evaluate** reasonably well.

In order to **improve**, the candidate could have explored the **similarities** and **differences** between marketing in consumer and industrial markets in **more depth**. Some parts of the answer could be more **specific** to the business to business market. The conclusion could summarise the reasons for saying that marketing is important in a business to business industrial market.

Here's a sample **mark scheme** for a 10 mark question:

Content	Application	Analysis	Evaluation
2 marks: Good understanding of industrial markets.	**2 marks**: Factors specific to the business applied in detail.	**2-3 marks**: Good use of relevant theory to analyse marketing in industrial and consumer markets.	**2-3 marks:** Judgement shown in considering the relevance of marketing to industrial markets.
1 mark: Some understanding shown of industrial markets.	**1 mark**: Some application to industrial sector.	**1 mark**: Limited use of theory.	**1 mark**: Some judgement shown in answer.

Answers to the Numerical Questions

Section One— Marketing

Page 7 — Marketing Analysis

Q1 (a)

Year	Quarter	Sales revenue (thousand £s)	4 quarter moving total	8 quarter moving total	Quarterly moving average
2001	1	630			
	2	567			
	3	552			605.63
	4	678	2427		605.88
2002	1	621	2418	4845	606.13
	2	578	2429	4847	595.25
	3	543	2420	4849	583.13
	4	600	2342	4762	577.25
2003	1	602	2323	4665	568.63
	2	550	2295	4618	558.50
	3	502	2254	4549	551.88
	4	560	2214	4468	
2004	1	589	2201	4415	

[14 marks]

(b)

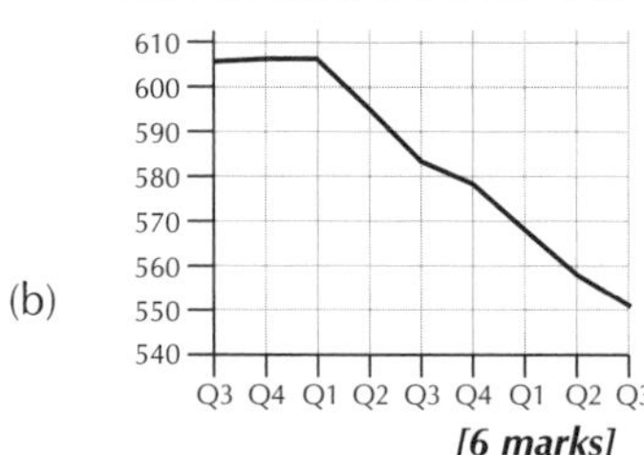

[6 marks]

Section Two — Accounting and Finance

Page 21 — Depreciation

Q2 Using straight line method, depreciation per year = (cost when new – cost when sold) ÷ amount of time owned.
Depreciation per year = (£2500 – £500) ÷ 4 = £500. ***[6 marks for correct answer and working]***

Page 27 — Financial Ratios

Q2 (a) Net profit ratio = net profit ÷ turnover ×100
Net profit ratio = (£750 000 – £250 000) ÷ £2 000 000 × 100 = 25%
[6 marks for correct answer and working]

Page 29 — Shareholder's Ratios

Q1 Dividend Yield = dividend per share ÷ price per share × 100
= 6p ÷ 300p × 100 = 2% ***[6 marks for correct answer and working]***

Page 31 — Contribution and Break Even Analysis

Q1 (a) Contribution = selling price – variable costs per unit
Contribution = £5 – £3 = £2
Break even output = fixed costs ÷ contribution
Break even output = £20 000 ÷ 2 = 10 000 units per year ***[6 marks for correct answer and working]***

Page 35 — Investment Appraisals

Q1 ARR = (average annual profit ÷ investment) × 100
Average annual profit = £100 000 – £60 000 = £40 000
ARR = £40 000 ÷ £200 000 × 100 = 20% ***[6 marks for correct answer and working]***

Page 37 — Investment Appraisals

Q1

	Cash inflow	Discount Value (5%)	Present Value
Year 1	£5K	0.952	£5K × 0.952 = £4760
Year 2	£5K	0.907	£5K × 0.907 = £4535
Year 3	£5K	0.864	£5K × 0.864 = £4320
Year 4	£5K	0.823	£5K × 0.823 = £4115
Year 5	£5K	0.784	£5K × 0.784 = £3920
Total Present Value of Cash Inflows			£21650
Net Present Value (total minus Investment)			-£17K = **£4650**

[8 marks in total:
3 marks for calculating all discount values correctly, 2 marks for calculating 3-4 values correctly, 1 mark for calculating 1-2 values.
2 marks for calculating all present values correctly, 1 mark for calculating 2-4 values correctly.
1 mark for adding present values correctly.
1 mark for working of net present value calculation.
1 mark for answer of £4650.]

Section Four — Operations Management

Page 61 — Critical Path Analysis

Q1

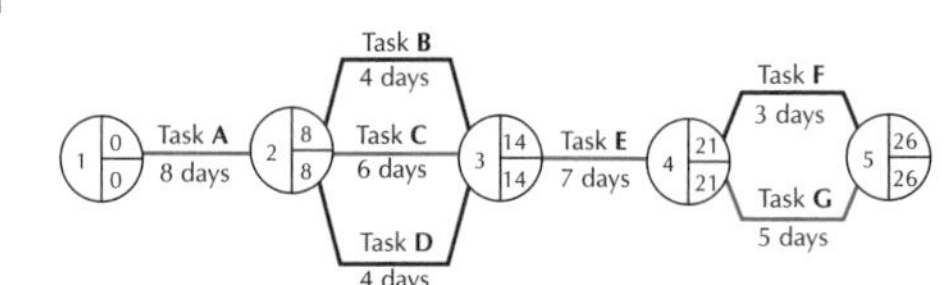

The project will take 26 days to complete.
[8 marks in total:
4 marks for putting (A), (B, C and D), (E), and (F and G) in the right order. 2 marks for one error. 1 mark for 2 errors.
1 mark for B C and D as simultaneous.
1 mark for F and G as simultaneous.
1 mark for the critical path — it's a thick pink line on the diagram.
1 mark for the total time — 26 days.]

Section Six — Objectives and Strategy

Page 93 — Decision Trees

Q1 (a)

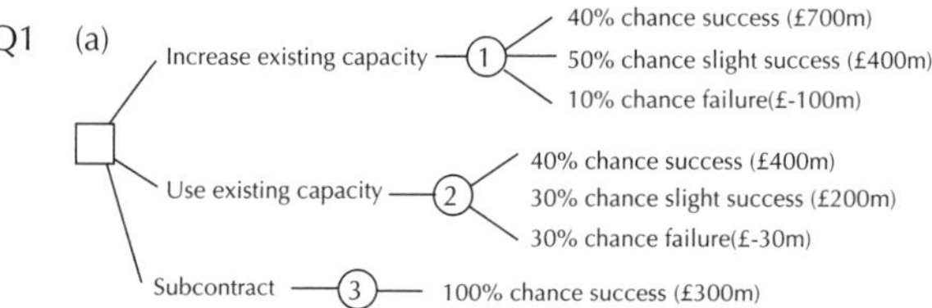

[2 marks for each correctly labelled probability and payoff]

(b) *Expected value at 1: £280m + £200m – £10m = £470m* ***[4 marks]****.*
Expected value at 2: £160m + £60m – £9m = £211m ***[4 marks]****.*
Expected value at 3: £300m ***[2 marks]****. Choosing and explaining the best option* ***[4 marks]****.*

Glossary

ACAS The Advisory, Conciliation and Arbitration Service, which acts as a mediator in industrial disputes.

assets Anything that provides a benefit to a business over a certain period of time.

balance sheet A snapshot of a firm's finances at a fixed point in time, showing assets and liabilities.

break-even analysis Shows the point where a company's total revenues equals their total costs.

budget Forecasts future earnings and future spending.

business cycle The regular pattern of growth and recession in the economy.

cashflow Money that comes into and goes out of a firm.

chain of command The number of hierarchical levels a communication or decision has to go through.

cost centre Part of a business that directly incurs costs.

critical path analysis Works out the quickest way to finish a set of tasks.

corporate culture The way a business does things — it affects the attitudes and expectations of employees.

current assets Things that are likely to be exchanged for cash within a year — e.g. stock, debtors.

debt factoring A service that pays a firm a cash advance of up to 80% of debts owed to that firm. The service then organises the collection of the debts and keeps the money themselves.

depreciation Losing value over time — fixed assets often depreciate.

diversification Expanding to produce new products or enter new markets.

elasticity of demand Shows the relationship between the price and demand of a product or service.

exchange rate The value of one currency in terms of another currency.

fiscal policy Government policy that sets tax rates and government spending.

fixed assets Things businesses keep for over a year — e.g. property, equipment, land, computers.

fixed costs Costs that stay the same — no matter how much a firm produces.

forecasting Trying to predict what will happen in the future.

gearing The proportion of a business financed through debt rather than equity.

GDP (gross domestic product) The total market share of goods and services produced by a country, within the country, over a period of time.

Human Resource Management (HRM) Looks after all the people aspects of a business — like hiring, firing and training.

inflation The increase in the price of goods and services.

interest rate Shows the cost of borrowing.

kaizen Japanese for "continuous improvement", used in quality control.

lean production Techniques that aim to reduce waste to an absolute minimum.

liabilities Debts a business owes.

liquidity How easily assets can be turned into cash.

marketing mix The four Ps firms use to market their goods / services — price, product, promotion and place.

market research Finding out about customers, markets and competitors.

merger Where two companies agree they should join together into one business.

mission statement A written description of a company's corporate objectives.

monetary policy Government policy that controls the interest rate — this affects inflation and exchange rates.

monopoly Where one firm controls most or all of the market share.

motivation Anything that makes you work harder and achieve more than normal.

multinational corporation A business with its headquarters in one country and bases in other countries.

operations management Planning and monitoring business operations to ensure they're as efficient as possible.

PEST analysis Used to analyse external opportunities and threats — looks at political, economic, social and technological issues.

private limited company (Ltd) A company that is owned by shareholders but its shares can't be sold on the stock market.

privatisation Selling publicly-owned companies to private individuals and firms.

productive efficiency How good a company is at turning inputs into outputs.

profit and loss account Statement showing how much money's gone into and out of a company over a period of time.

profit centre Part of a business that directly generates revenue.

protectionism When a country tries to protect its own companies by making it harder for foreign companies to trade in that country.

public limited company (PLC) A company that is owned by shareholders and its shares can be sold on the stock market.

return on capital employed (ROCE) Shows you how much money is made by the business compared to how much money's been put into the business.

social responsibility The responsibilities a firm has to its employees, customers and other stakeholders.

span of control The number of staff working under one manager.

stakeholders All the people affected by a business — workers, shareholders, customers and the public.

SWOT analysis Used to determine business strategy — looks at the strengths, weaknesses, opportunities and threats facing the firm.

takeover Where one firm buys over 50% of the shares of another firm, giving them the controlling interest.

trade unions Groups that act on behalf of groups of employees in talks with their employer.

variable costs Costs that vary, depending on what business the firm does.

working capital Money available to fund day-to-day spending.

Index

Index

Index